ABOUT THE AUTHOR

Born in Pakistan, Khalid Aziz enjoyed a first career in the media, working initially for the BBC and then ITV and Channel 4. He founded The Aziz Corporation in 1983 and the company has grown to be Britain's leading specialist in spoken communications. Khalid himself has tutored hundreds of senior business people and politicians and the methodology he created is now applied extensively by Aziz Corporation consultants. He is a holder of the BP/Industrial Society Industrial Journalist of the Year Award. In 1997, he was appointed a Lieutenant of the Royal Victorian Order (LVO) for services to The Prince's Trust. He is married and lives in Hampshire, England where he is a Deputy Lieutenant (DL). This is his tenth book.

Presenting to Win

A Guide for Finance and Business Professionals

Khalid Aziz

Oak Tree Press
Dublin

Oak Tree Press
Merrion Building
Lower Merrion Street
Dublin 2, Ireland
http://www.oaktreepress.com

A catalogue record of this book is
available from the British Library.

ISBN 1 86076 135 6

Printed in Britain
Biddles Ltd., Guildford and King's Lynn

CONTENTS

PART THREE
INTERNAL PRESENTATIONS

ACKNOWLEDGEMENTS

I would like to thank all The Aziz Corporation consultants, but particularly:

Anne Blamey for her input on voice development and Pamela Jack for her advice on style. Steve Hudson has been the backbone of our technical services almost since the inception of the company and also helps maintain the quality of our service. Mike Robinson and Peter Ruff have over several years worked with me to help hone and refine our methodology.

I would like to thank our support team, Linda Mackenzie, Lynsay Bignell, Adam Galfskiy, Kim Kemp, Claire Lidstone, Mark Lidstone and Sue McGill.

My thanks to David Givens for his forbearance, Brian Langan for his intelligent editing of the manuscript and everyone at Oak Tree who has worked on this book.

I would also like to thank Maureen Lidstone for typing the original drafts of the manuscript.

Finally, I would like to thank all of our loyal clients over the years, who of course have been the key to our success.

Khalid Aziz
West Stratton
November 1999

To my family, and especially my children:

To Robert, who is beginning to learn
the value of effective presentation

To Charlotte, for whom image is the key to presentation

To Fleur, who presents from the heart

To Nadira, who is just beginning to understand her audiences

And finally to my wife, Kim, the best presenter I know,
which is why everyone loves her.

INTRODUCTION

It has got to stop. The average business presentation made in the English-speaking world today is woeful and we just cannot go on this way. Not that it is much better in other countries where business takes itself seriously. Ironically, in the UK, the birthplace of the English language, business presentations are generally as bad as you will find anywhere.

Why is it that the spoken word does not receive the same amount of attention and promotion compared to the written word? Well, our media, even the electronic media, is still dominated by arts graduates from universities, where there is still a prevailing view that the job of academia is to save their charges from the world of business and all that goes with it. True, they do steep the heads of their students in words, but these are predominantly written words. Where is the art of declamation? Where is there real debate, where it is permissible to hold a view and argue it strongly for the sake of debate, where even the speaker may not automatically agree with the standpoint he or she is promoting? Where is the oratory?

It is little wonder then that when graduates find themselves in business, they struggle to make themselves understood. Not that they have great role models to look up to. As a rule, their bosses struggle too.

> "I make good presentations and bad presentations. The trouble is, I don't know why the good presentations are good or indeed why the bad presentations are bad."

Such is the cry of many a business presenter who comes to see us for advice on how to present effectively.

It used to be in business that you could avoid making presentations, hiding in the undergrowth created by those more keen on making a name for themselves. After all, you were hired for your intelligence, for your technical expertise and of course for your management ability. Talking a lot, by definition, does not go hand-in-hand with strong, silent and decisive management. I have come across scores of very senior managers who have risen and vanished without trace, making very few presentations — clearly risk-averse types who keep their noses clean in the hope of hanging their hat on a pension.

Take the gent in his mid-60s who, after an illustrious career in the upper echelons of industry, was cruising comfortably with a nice portfolio of blue chip non-executive directorships. Then one day the chairman of one of the companies he served had a brainwave. How would he like to stand up at the forthcoming AGM in his role as chairman of the remuneration committee and explain the new executive share option scheme to the shareholders? The request was given added piquancy by the fact that the company concerned was a newly privatised utility. Unfortunately, the request did not come with a multiple-choice answer. When the individual concerned arrived with us he had two weeks to get his act together. He had never spoken in public before. He applied himself and did passably well. But how much better would it have been for his company (and his stress levels) if speaking ability had been just another tool in his executive armoury acquired early on, along with all his other executive skills as he was progressing up the corporate ladder?

When people pop out towards the top of the business world, making presentations usually comes as a shock to the system. Little wonder then that in a survey, 76 per cent of people said that standing up in public and making a presentation is the most daunting thing required of them in business life.

The trouble is, many people delude themselves about their real abilities. It is rather like the theory of a publican friend of mine. The trouble with his business, he believes, is that everyone knows how to drink, therefore everyone thinks they know how to run a pub. It is the same with speaking. The ability to open one's mouth and talk does not automatically mean that one is a brilliant speaker.

Sadly, the evidence of this lack of ability is there to be seen. And it often manifests itself in disaster. Oh, how one's heart sinks when a clearly ill-prepared presenter arrives to speak with a huge pile of overheads! Often they compound the issue either by apologising for not being the right person to make the presentation or by confessing that due to pressure of work, they have had "little time to prepare".

This book takes the mystique out of presentation. It is designed for those who *know* they need to present more effectively. Whether you make presentations every day or have never presented in your life but know the fateful day is coming, this book is for you. But what about your time? We all know that presentations are hugely time-consuming, even if you have some idea about what it is you want to say. This book will actually save you time. Following the methodologies outlined here, it should be possible to prepare a ten-minute presentation in just half an hour. I hope that is a reasonable payback on your time. How long will it take to improve? With a little application, you can use the information to good effect and become a stunning speaker in just six weeks! So please read on and enjoy. You are about to break the final frontier in business — that of effective spoken communication.

PART ONE
Presentation Fundamentals

Chapter 1

THE THEORY OF EFFECTIVE SPOKEN COMMUNICATIONS

Most people would regard a successful communication as one that "gets the message across". Whilst this is true, it is not the whole story. In business, a successful communication has to go much further. Not only does the message have to be put across, but the audience also has to react positively to that message.

In short, we can sum up the definition of a successful communication as:

> "One which modifies the behaviour of the audience so that they do something in your favour that they would not have done had you not spoken to them."

I will look at this definition and its implications for presentations later in this chapter. But first, I will examine the differences between the written and the spoken word.

Essential Differences between the Written and Spoken Word

Before we can contemplate making any effective spoken communication, we have to understand that there are essential differences between the written and spoken word. In most educational establishments in the western world, the emphasis is placed on the written word over the spoken word as evidence of scholarly achievement. This is almost ingrained in our culture and in particular is reinforced by teaching methods.

From the moment we can talk we are told to shut up and listen. When we go to school the valued part of what we do is normally in writing. If you talk a lot, you are condemned as a chatterbox and punished accordingly. Early examinations are all in writing. At university, most of the exams are in writing. If at university you are invited to do a *viva voce*, or oral exam, it is almost as a punishment for not getting the written exam right!

In this way, people's natural spoken communications ability has almost been educated out of them, which is a tragedy, because increasingly in certain areas of business life, the written word is becoming subservient in importance to the words we speak.

In the English language, words are spoken on average at the rate of three words per second; that is, 180 words a minute. Of course, some people are able to speak much faster than that. You may have seen and heard on television the tobacco auctioneers in Virginia whose patter is unintelligible except to those who have become attuned to their rapid-fire delivery over a period of several years. On British television, the doyen of the BBC's astronomy programme *The Sky at Night* is a delightful septuagenarian called Patrick Moore. He is noted for speaking rather faster than the norm, at around five or six words a second, but of course the intelligibility of what he says decreases. There is no doubt that after several minutes of listening to such a rapid delivery, the listener can become more than a little weary.

On the other hand there is another famous broadcaster, Alistair Cooke with his *Letter from America* — another BBC programme, this time on radio — who specialises in delivering the English language at a speed of far less than three words a second. He manages to make a script, which for most people would be 10 minutes' worth of broadcasting, last 15 minutes. A clever technique if you are being paid by the minute!

Whilst I bow to no one in my admiration of Alistair Cooke and his delivery, as indeed I do to Patrick Moore, these departures from the norm are just that. For ordinary speech as it is normally spoken in everyday life and indeed on television in news programmes, three words a second seems to be the speed at which the English language can be picked up intelligibly over a long period of time.

By contrast, the written word can be read far more quickly than three words a second. Tests have shown that an educated person can pick up words intelligibly from a printed page at up to 15 words a second. Interestingly, that speed goes right down as soon as figures are inserted in the text. This is because the brain has to go through extra processes of cognition in order to translate the figures into concepts that the mind can cope with.

If you doubt the speed at which we are able to read text in our mind, think back to your school days when you learned to read. Initially you started off by recognising single syllable words through pointing at them and saying them out loud. You then moved on to larger, multi-syllable words. From there came progression to reading whole lines of text at a time, often helped by placing a piece of card under each line and sliding the card down as you completed each sentence.

In the initial stages, you were reading aloud until the speed increased to the point at which the sound ceased to come from your mouth. Then you got rid of the card and simply mouthed the words that you saw on the page. Finally, realising that your mouth would not move as fast as your eyes could take in the words and the brain could translate them, you found yourself reading in your head.

So we can see that, in terms of the number of words that can be transmitted in any given length of time, speech when compared to the written word is inefficient by a factor of up to five times — three words a second compared with fifteen words a second.

It is also important to appreciate the way in which our brains work and the relationship between the brain and the mouth. Picture, if you will, your brain as a personal computer and your mouth as an output device — rather like a printer, to continue the computer analogy.

Just think how the human brain has developed over the last century or so. A hundred years ago, hardly anybody used a telephone. Today, it's not unusual for people in a business environment to be on two telephone calls simultaneously. Clearly, our brains have developed and accelerated through extra use. If you like, again in computer terms, we have developed Pentium III brains. However, the output device, the mouth, is still tied to 50,000-year-old technology and is based on the original caveman's requirement to say "Ug!" The mouth as an output device is necessarily very slow because of the need to articulate each word clearly. The language we use today is still as slow and deliberate as it ever was, with little scope for cramming more words into each and every spoken second.

More importantly, there is a fundamental difference between the way in which the brain works and the way in which the mouth works. We can *think* about a number of different things all at once. In computer terms, this is known as concurrent processing. However, your mouth is essentially a linear device; that is, you can only *speak* one word after another. Therefore, whilst you think concurrently, you have to speak in a way that ensures that what you say has a beginning, a middle and an end. The challenge is to begin at the beginning, to ensure that you get an understandable flow of information, that is neither jumbled nor confusing, coming out of your mouth.

Next we have to look at the *impact* of the spoken word. In the late 1950s, a Californian college professor called Albert Mehrabian carried out a study of the effectiveness of face-to-face spoken communications and concluded that just seven per cent of the communications' effectiveness was down to the words themselves. The rest of the effectiveness could be explained in terms of the images of the individual doing the presentation, body language, tone of voice, speed of delivery and so on.

Mehrabian carried out his tests with college students, so it is arguable that people in their late teens and early 20s might be more fixated on image rather than words. More recent tests conducted in business environments have indicated that words are more important than was shown by Mehrabian's studies. But even here, they account for only about 40 per cent of the effectiveness of a spoken communication — so let us stick with that figure. We can then see that the rate of three words a second is effectively only one and a half words a second because of this inefficiency.

Additionally, a further setback is that, for a reader of the written word, it is possible when reaching the end of a sentence, a paragraph or a page that has not been fully understood to go back and re-read and re-interpret what has been said. Clearly, someone listening live to a spoken presentation has no such opportunity to review what has been said. So the burden is all on the speaker to put in artificial recaps in order to bring the listener up to date. Indeed, it is said that one of the key methods of presentation still employed by armies throughout the world is to get the men fell in, tell them what you are going to say, and then say it, and then tell them what you said! In effect, you repeat everything twice to ensure that the message has got through.

This is not a bad methodology, particularly where the precise communication of instructions is required. If we accept the principle of this repetition, we can see that, effectively, three words a second comes down to just one word a second because of the double repeat. And remember, less than half of the communication will be understood!

All this serves to prove that speech is a highly inefficient medium when compared to the written word. But matters don't rest there. Because of this ability to go back and re-read what you have just read, it is possible with the written word to discourse in sweeping generalisations and concepts. This is because the reader can slow down and analyse the underlying meaning of broad conceptualisations in order to fully understand them. However, with the spoken word, one has to give examples and be much more specific about what it is you are trying to say. In other words, with the spoken word, it is vital to tell stories to illustrate the points you are trying to get across.

The reason for this is almost genetic. It is only since the turn of the century that we have had, and then only in the western world, anything approaching universal adult literacy. Despite the fact that Caxton invented the printing press and Gutenberg subsequently invented moveable type, the world of print and writing was still, up to the late 1900s, very much in the hands of an elite.

Indeed, 20 years ago, it was said in the UK that six million adults were functionally illiterate, which meant that they could not be put into a hazardous workplace, because they would not be able to read warning signs on machinery. As we enter the new millennium, that figure has grown to something like nine million functionally illiterate adults in the UK. Sadly, things are getting worse, not better!

However, the oral tradition goes back thousands of years, almost to the birth of man, and it is all based on storytelling. Indeed, the early great books that were written down — the Ramayana, the Vedas, the Torah, the Bible, the Koran — are all based on stories. They are written in narrative form, they are very specific. Indeed, if we look at the great communicators and teachers of the past and present, they have been and are the ones who talk in terms of stories and are very specific in illustrating their arguments. Talking in parables has always been a powerful communications tool. There is a very real sense in which, psychologically, we use narrative to put order on a chaotic world. The trouble with stories is that, again, they take time, eating into the valuable space available to the potential receivers of your pearls of wisdom.

And if that was not enough, there's another huge drawback, which is the attention span of your audience. It is said that in the western world today, thanks largely to the influence of television, the average attention span is just three and a quarter minutes. This means that the effective speaker has to continually attract the audience's attention. This is achieved principally through interaction. The interactive approach to spoken communication is relatively new.

There are people alive today who can just about remember how during general elections politicians used to stand on the hustings at street corners. From these elevated wooden structures they would make speeches lasting for several hours, and be sure of a great audience from those who had nothing else to do with their time (admittedly this was before the invention of television and indeed radio). Mostly, these speeches were didactic in their delivery style, simple one-way communications handing down "tablets of stone"; in those days, the audience would happily stand around and lap up the message. Today, because there is so much competition for our attention, it is a very brave speaker indeed who ignores the need for interactivity.

Interactivity can be anything from getting a laugh, asking a question for a show of hands or simply achieving some kind of acknowledgement that the audience is still alive and following your train of thought. It is a vital part of any effective spoken communication in a modern environment. The trouble is, interactivity again takes time.

What we are seeing from all the above is that, when compared to the written word, speech is hugely inefficient. So why in this world of e-mails and faxes do we still bother with the spoken word? Why is it that the airlines are not out of business but instead booming, relying as they do on business people flying around the world for face-to-face meetings with existing clients and new prospects?

The answer is that there is one thing you can do much more effectively with the spoken word that cannot be so easily delivered with the written word. You can create an *impact*. Impact has a daughter word, which is *passion*. A spoken communication without impact and passion is rather like an egg without salt. It's all there, the content is right, it is nutritious but it just doesn't taste so good. I could almost say that reading this book will improve your sex life — because it will make you more passionate! If you think about it, even pillow talk, carried out successfully, fulfils the definition of a successful communication — "One which modifies the behaviour of the audience so that they do something in your favour that they would not have done had you not spoken to them"!!

In a world where there are so many communications coming at a potential listener, would-be great speakers ignore impact and passion at their peril. Indeed, we would go further and suggest that if you are incapable of being passionate about your subject, you have no business speaking on it. Essentially, all presentations are to a greater or lesser extent sales exercises. No one will be convinced to buy from you unless they are convinced that you are convinced yourself. They will only see this if you are clearly passionate about what you are saying.

Message, Audience and Medium

When embarking on any kind of presentation, there are three key elements that must be borne in mind: firstly, the *message* that you want to get across; secondly, the *audience* to whom you want to get the message across; and finally, the *medium*. The medium indicates the kind of environment in which you are making your presentation. This can vary from a one-to-one presentation across the table to a semi-formal boardroom presentation, right up to a fully fledged formal presentation in front of an audience ranging from 20 to 200, even to 2,000.

The Audience

Of those three key criteria — message, audience, medium — one is paramount when embarking on any presentation. That is the audience, and the analysis of that audience, which is the most critical factor to the success of any presentation. There are many reasons for this and to appreciate those reasons, it is vital first of all to understand what makes for a successful spoken communication. Look again at the definition of a successful communication given at the beginning of this chapter:

> "One which modifies the behaviour of the audience so that they do something in your favour that they would not have done had you not spoken to them."

Let us analyse that in more detail. Clearly, you have to have a message that you want to get across. However, even if you are successful in getting that message across, but the audience does not *do* something — that is, you do not modify their behaviour — then the message will have been wasted. It is important that your communication is such that you get action from the audience and, in particular, that action must be *in your favour*.

For example, you can put the same message across to two different audiences and receive a completely different reaction. Let us say, for instance, that you are the manager of a division that employs, say, 100 people. One day you come in and, knowing the pressure that your company is under to trim costs and contain headcount, you look very carefully at your staff numbers and conclude that they can be cut. Through careful analysis, you work out that you could reduce your staff numbers from 100 to 75 — a 25 per cent reduction.

You go along to your boss and say, "Great news! I can reduce our headcount by 25 per cent and still maintain efficiency."

The reaction of your boss is likely to be positive, coupled no doubt with a suggestion that it would be good if you could achieve the dirty deed by Friday. Indeed, in many companies, whole careers have been built on such an ability to scythe through manpower. Clearly, in this instance your message has got a positive response from your audience and they are going to do something in your favour (either through a pay rise or share options or other such bonus) that they would not have done had you not spoken to them.

So, flushed with the success of the transmission of this message to your boss, you get your workforce gathered together in one room and you give them the good news. Picture the scene. You stand up in front of them and say, "Good news! I can end the speculation about redundancies. There will be some. In fact, by Friday, 25 of you will not be working for us any longer. And there's even better news — the department will maintain its efficiency."

Same message, different audience — but what is their reaction likely to be?

This stark example clearly indicates how you can communicate an identical message to two separate audiences and have a completely different response.

Another reason why audience analysis is most critical at the beginning of any spoken communication process is borne out by the experience of listening to a presenter who has not understood his or her audience. We have all been in situations where the presenter has clearly not engaged from the very start and their words have gone right over the heads of the audience and been ignored. In the worst instances, the presenter fails to notice this and blunders on willy-nilly. The whole presentation is a disaster, resulting in, at best, an attitude of indifference from the audience; at worst, nothing short of hostility.

For this reason, the first question that has to be asked when contemplating a presentation or any kind of spoken communication is:

Who is the audience?

The next question to be asked is:

What do they want to hear?

Clarifying the expectations of the audience is critical. What you are dealing with here is two bodies of knowledge. There is what *you* want to say and what *they*, the audience, want to hear. Of course, what you want to say will not always be what they want to hear, and what they want to hear will not always be what you want to say. Usually, there is a trade-off between the two. Again, if we look at the example above of a communication between yourself and the people who work for you, there will be clear differences of view between what you want to say and what they want to hear.

Let's take another example. In another communication with your workforce, you may want to say that you want them to work twice as hard for half the amount of pay. They might prefer to hear that they will actually get twice the amount of pay for half the amount of work. Somehow, you have to find a suitable compromise between the two.

The Message

Remember what I said about the link between your brain and your mouth? In order to avoid mouthing complete rubbish, you need to think carefully about what you want to say, giving it a clear beginning, middle and end.

What you have to do therefore is analyse the audience; who are they, what do they want to hear. Then you have to work out what it is that *you* want to say. So that is our third question when contemplating a spoken communication:

What do you want to say?

Once you have worked out the answers to the first three key questions, look for the overlap between what it is that you want to say and what the audience wants to hear. It is at this point that you start your presentation. In doing this, you are obeying one of the essential tenets of human communication. It is most starkly seen in negotiations. All good negotiations are designed to end with a so-called win/win solution. To achieve this win/win objective, the starting point of all negotiations has to be to establish the common ground; that is, the ground on which both sides can agree. It is exactly the same with spoken communications; you start off playing to the common ground. This, of course, is exactly what successful politicians do.

Finding the Overlap

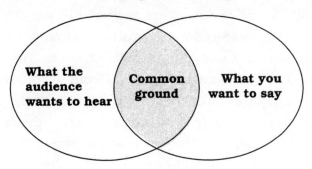

A successful politician is someone who can go into a room, speak for an hour, and after an hour have people saying, "That was fantastic! I would follow him over a cliff." However, when asked the simple question, "What did he actually say?", the response of the admirer is more often than not, "I don't know what he said, but I'd follow him over a cliff."

Of course, what the politician has done is to make each individual in that room feel very special, that he or she has understood what's important for them. In other words, each person leaves the meeting feeling they have been personally touched by the politician. This has to be used with care; there are legion stories of politicians overcooking it. Even experienced speakers can come unstuck. However, it is a powerful technique and as long as you are sincere and do your research properly, it will serve you well in your presentation.

In reality, what you are doing is harnessing a well-known psychological phenomenon known as *"mirroring"*. Mirroring is a phenomenon that affects not only human beings but also higher primates. A good example of this was in the film *Gorillas in the Mist*, a biopic of Dianne Fossey (played by Sigourney Weaver) who had a fascination for gorillas and eventually became an expert on the subject, before her untimely and gruesome death in a machete attack.

According to the film, when Fossey was about to encounter her first gorillas in Rwanda, she was given two pieces of advice by her ranger guide. Firstly, never run away from a gorilla — a policy which is easy to state but difficult to put into practice when a 12-foot-high gorilla rears up in front of you and beats its chest. Having run away the first time, she was reminded of the second piece of advice, which was to mirror the actions of the gorillas. So, gathering up her courage, she crept up close to the family of gorillas and observed what they were doing. They were eating leaves, so Fossey pretended that she was eating leaves. One of the gorillas had a scratch, so Fossey had a scratch. By continuing to mirror the activities of the animals, eventually the gorillas looked at her and thought, "Well, here's another gorilla", or at least someone who was like them. From that point on, the gorillas and Fossey became firm friends. This mirroring technique is similar to that used by human beings, although often the signals used to mirror can be much more subtle and difficult for the untrained eye to interpret. However, most mirroring signals are picked up at the subconscious level.

Another way of understanding the technique of mirroring is to think of yourself as one of a pair of dice, the other being the audience. Your agenda may, so to speak, be represented by the six-spot side of the dice. However, if the audience is showing you three spots (which you have ascertained through advance audience analysis), then you must start off showing them three spots. If you start off your communication in this way, there will be instant rapport — instant communication. Once communication has been established, you can rotate to four spots and because mirroring is a two-way process, they will rotate to four spots. You then go to five, they go to five; you turn to six spots and they will turn to six spots. You will then have shifted the agenda and moved the overlap. In effect, you will be communicating on your agenda.

CASE STUDY — J MAYS

Engage your audience by celebrating their enthusiasms

Making a speech to open a stylishly assembled art exhibition at the Royal College of Art, celebrating 30 years of vehicle design, it is difficult to compete with an environment full of flashy cars. It is an even bigger challenge to a designer. After all, designers express themselves principally on paper rather than with the spoken word. It becomes even more difficult when you have invited 300-plus people to the exhibition opening and then crammed them into a low-ceilinged room already preheated by muggy outside temperatures in the 80s and augmented by arc lights playing on the exhibits.

That was the task that befell J. Mays, Head of Design for Ford Global. He is the man who is responsible ultimately for the shapes of one of the most popular brands of cars in the world.

It would have been easy to go on and on about how Ford had been sponsoring design at the RCA for the last 30 years, but mercifully J. Mays kept his comments to a crisp five minutes. He was good too, proving that in any area an expert who can communicate effectively will rise and rise. He quickly engaged his audience — primarily design students and graduates — by assuring them that he understood where everybody stood when it came to cars. "If you take one thing away from this exhibition, it should be this," he said. "Nothing handles like a rental car!" — thus assuring us he wasn't a boring designer but had a little more about him.

He then went on to hit us with his message — unsurprisingly, that design was "a good thing". But he did it so enthusiastically and with so much passion that it really did make all the difference between an ordinary opening speech and a really stunning one.

What is more, he really touched their collective nerves when he reminded them with an insight into the human psyche that, "When you see someone in their home, that is how they are. When you see them in a car, that is how they would like to be."

Students of any kind are not notably open to over-enthusiasm for someone twice their age speaking to them in a hot and sticky room, but they whooped and cheered at the end. He had moved them.

Key Lesson*: Judge your audience's interests, and mirror your style according to what they would like to hear, gradually shifting the agenda until you have got across your message.*

Mirroring is a highly successful way of ensuring effective communication. However, suppose your agenda is six spots and through audience analysis you understand that they are going to be showing you what amounts to one spot. If you come in at six while they are at one, there will be no overlap. There will be no form of communication and you will fail to get through to your audience.

So, in summary, what needs to happen before any proposed presentation? Firstly you must start with the key question:

Who is the audience?

Followed by the second key question:

What do they want to hear?

Once you have established the answers to those questions, you then need to ask yourself:

What do I want to say?

You then need to develop a clear idea of how you will measure the success of your communication, remembering that you're *trying to get them to do something in your favour that they would not have done had you not spoken to them*. Once you have done that, you will be well on the way to starting your communication.

The starting point for any communication is the overlap between what you want to say and what the audience wants to hear. By establishing this through the processes outlined above, you have overcome one of the most difficult steps in any presentation — namely, getting started. The rest should flow much more easily.

The Medium

So, we have dealt with the audience and we have dealt with the message. We now need to consider the selection of the correct *medium*.

In terms of normal presentations, when we speak of the medium, we are really talking about the environment in which we are giving our presentation. This is very dependent on the numbers of people who make up the audience for the presentation. However, most people tend to think of presentations as formal affairs, often involving a platform, a microphone, and in some cases, lights. Many people insist that they make no real presentations at all, relying instead on what they describe as "informal" presentations.

The majority of presentations in the business environment usually fall into the category of "informal". Usually, they are to fewer than half a dozen people and yet the numbers of such presentations taken together form a significant part of presentational activity — usually much more than so-called formal presentations. Paradoxically, these informal presentations are in fact the trickiest, because whilst you may hope that the guard of the audience is down, so is that of the speaker. All too often, "informal" can be an excuse for not taking the presentation seriously, often with disastrous results. There are many stories of individuals who, for example, when going through a rigorous selection procedure for a new job, have acquitted themselves well in the formal interview, only to fall apart when they allow their guard to drop in an informal setting.

The reality is that, formal or informal, all presentations require a similar approach. There are, however, some clear differences and these are principally to do with the environment in which you find yourself — the medium.

For example, in so-called informal presentations, it might be far better to do away with complex computer graphics and 35mm slides and instead make use of a small flip-chart type presenter to illustrate your presentation. Clearly, such a visual aid would be totally out of place if you were standing up in front a hall of 500 people. Similarly, the use of overhead projectors needs to be watched very carefully. We will discuss visual aids in more detail later in the book.

Another question frequently asked about "small environment" presentations is, "Do I stand or sit?" This very much depends on the perceived formality or informality of the occasion and also the numbers of people present. For example, it would be ridiculous to stand and give a presentation to one or two people, but perhaps appropriate to stand if there are more than, say, six or seven people. Much will depend also on the shape and layout of the room that you are presenting in and indeed your own physical stature. I have known very tall and very short people who prefer to give seated presentations for completely different reasons: tall people often do not want to appear domineering and short people often do not want to highlight their lack of stature.

How you treat the medium obviously depends on your own particular views and the environment itself. Often, that environment cannot be determined by you. It is more often than not dictated by those who have invited you to present. If you can, enquire in advance about the layout out of the room so that it does not come as a total surprise. Additionally, if possible, turn up in advance of your presentation to check the layout and any equipment you might need to use. If you are unable to do this, you will just have to be adept at thinking on your feet and adapting to the environment in which you find yourself.

Whilst the above factors do impact on the effectiveness of a presentation, of the three key factors to contemplate before embarking on a presentation, the medium is the least critical when compared to the audience and the message. The approach to all presentations, large or small, formal or informal, should be the same. The big danger is to believe that a short, informal presentation means an easier presentation.

Key Points to Remember

- Speech takes longer to absorb than written text, and you should tailor your presentation accordingly.

- Hold your audience's attention through interactivity.

- Speak with impact and passion.

- The three key elements of spoken communication are message, medium and audience.

- The effectiveness of your spoken communication will be measured by the audience doing something in your favour that they would not have done had you not spoken to them.

- There are four basic questions to ask yourself before any type of presentation:

- *Who are your audience?*

- ◆ *What do they want to hear?*

- ◆ *What is it you want to say?*

- ◆ *Where is the overlap?*

- Presentations can be either formal or informal, but the key questions remain the same.

- The same message might get a different reaction from a different audience.

- Mirror the audience, gradually tipping the agenda towards your message.

Chapter 2

THEORY INTO PRACTICE (1): ORGANISING THE CONTENT

In this chapter, we are going to look in more depth at the construction of a presentation. Clearly, getting the message right is critical. We have already discussed the fact that this message has to be tailored to the particular audience you are addressing. Before we can continue with developing the content of our presentation, it is important to understand that there are some key differences in the construction of a spoken presentation when compared to that of a written presentation (see also Chapter 1). Many spoken presentations fail through lack of understanding of these differences, leading to the production of a presentation that is turgid in content and that inevitably comes across as boring and uninteresting.

Let us first consider what might happen if you are asked to write a written report on a given subject. How might you go about it? The process normally goes something like this. First you set out the background to the report. Then you might discuss the methodology that you used to research the subject. You might then follow this up with the results of your research and then finally would come, as it were, the "cherry on the cake" — the conclusions and recommended actions. The process might be best illustrated as below:

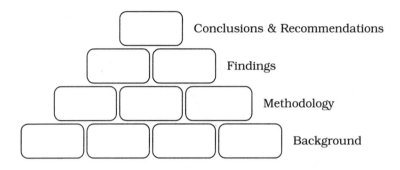

This empirical approach — building the content up block-by-block — is perfectly justified in a written report. It is logical and creates a well-ordered structure for the content. If the reader needs to find the report's conclusions straight away, they simply have to turn to the end of the document. Indeed, many financial analysts advise that when reading a company's annual report you start at the back and then work your way to the front. Although this is principally because the notes to the accounts are often more interesting than the accounts themselves, it is a useful discipline to apply to other forms of report.

Effective spoken communications are constructed in completely the opposite way to written reports. They start off with the conclusions in order to grab the attention of the audience and then move on to flesh out those key points with the details of how the conclusions were reached. Of course, an executive summary at the start of a written report — including an outline of the conclusions — or a strong introductory chapter, acts in much the same way, grabbing the attention of the reader. This is a welcome but relatively recent development in written reports, and in fact it probably draws on the experience of the spoken word.

We see this "attention grabbing" every night when we watch television news. The bulletins always lead with a set of headlines which are designed not only to give the main points of the news in descending importance but also to dangle the car-

rot of an interesting snippet which, although often insignifi-
cant, will keep you watching. The use of headlines is critical in
addressing another golden rule in the world of spoken communications:

Just because the audience is in the room
does not mean that they are listening to you.

In other words, you have to grab the attention of your audience. All successful spoken communications start with, in one
form of words or another, "Hey, guess what?" People are simply not attuned to listening to a slow build-up of background
methodology followed by results and then the final conclusions. When listening to a presentation, what a listener wants
is the conclusion first so they can decide whether it is worth
continuing to listen. Only when you have hooked your audience with a key fact can you then go into the background to
substantiate the conclusion and recommendations.

To gain a greater understanding of this key difference, let
us look at news bulletins again. As we have already mentioned, they always start with headlines. The overall objective
of a headline is to ensure that the viewer or listener stays listening to or watching the particular radio station or TV channel. The headlines also serve to stimulate the interest of the
audience in such a way that they will listen more actively to
what is being said. Advertising, particularly in print, works in
much the same way.

All well and good, but what is a powerful headline? Arguably, two of the greatest motivators in life are sex and money.
You may, in the course of normal business presentations,
have little opportunity to offer much by way of the former, but
when it comes to money, there is almost always some kind of
angle you can develop in order to interest your audience. For
example, an internal presentation to superiors inevitably leads
to the demand for allocation of resources or the application of

capital. All too often, such presentations build up to the final figure. In other words, the audience of decision-makers has to wait until the end to hear what they are most interested in. Why not confront that issue right up front and give the price tag and the benefits of the investment you are inviting your audience to commit to, in easy-to-understand monetary terms?

CASE STUDY — CRAIG BARRETT (PRESIDENT OF INTEL)

Stunning facts which hit the audience between the eyes can help lift a presentation

If you want to know about computers, ask a nerd. You know the type — under 25, baggy T-shirt, lots of spots. What can an old grey fox three times that age tell you? Well, quite a lot actually, if his name is Craig Barrett, President of the Intel Corporation. Just a couple of months short of his sixtieth birthday, he held his audience enthralled at the Wall Street Journal's sixth annual CEOs' summit in London with his account of where we were headed on the Internet.

After a slightly shaky start, it looked as if we were in for the usual Chief Executive guff — high on platitudes, low on facts and new information. But he surprised us, progressing well and despite his relaxed style hammering home his basic message: that if you are not in e-commerce in five years' time, you probably won't be in business.

Having grabbed us with this bold headline, he had impressive figures to back up his view. For example, it took 38 years to sell 50 million radio sets but just four years to achieve the same number of Internet subscribers.

He pressed home other messages too; the principal one being that we must lobby government to ensure that we have enough bandwidth to support the explosion in Internet traffic.

"Bits," he said, "are the oil of the Internet economy. If we don't have enough of it, then we will not be able to exploit it to the full." Interestingly, the US and Japan are way ahead on this with Britain and Europe languishing behind particularly when it comes to the cost of Internet access.

Another stunning fact was the revelation that Intel Corporation took its first order on the Internet in July 1998. Just a year later, they were doing a billion dollars worth of Internet business a month.

Did he get anything wrong? Well I could have done with simpler, less busy graphics, but the demonstrations of the innovations in computer processing power were efficiently conducted and clearly well rehearsed without coming across as slick. Sadly, Mr Barrett was not as well served by the video-switching and the video itself, which were out of sync.

In the field of high tech, there is a feeling that you are very much over the hill by 30. But the Intel President is living proof that it ain't necessarily so. You just have to have a user friendly interface which helps ordinary mortals understand what on earth is going on in the world of computers. Craig Barrett proved you can teach an old dog new tricks.

Key Lesson: *Striking headlines backed up with solid facts will win over an audience every time.*

When you have decided what you want to say, you must find the most powerful headline and pull it up front, even though you may be repeating it again somewhere in the body of the text. Quite often when preparing a presentation, it is hard to find this headline. This is usually because you are too close to both the subject and the presentation itself. In other words, you often cannot see the wood for the trees. Even assuming you have picked up on a key financial aspect within your presentation, you may find it almost impossible, until you have gained some experience in the process, to spot a key financial headline. Rehearsing the presentation in front of someone can be extremely helpful. If possible, this person should be drawn from as close to the target audience as possible. Coming to the presentation fresh and with knowledge of what the audience is expecting to hear and of what will motivate them should mean they will be able to help you fillet out the key motivator in headline form and put it at the top. The key question to ask yourself and the person with whom you are consulting is:

What will really make this audience sit up and listen?

In short, you have to tell them as early as possible exactly what is in it for them. As you move into the body of your presentation, remember that it is vital if you are to retain the interest of the audience to present benefits and not just features. All too often, presenters overlook this vital area of influencing skill. Understanding the relationship between features and benefits is a major plank in the world of marketing. It is worth looking at this in more detail.

Benefits and Features

If, for example, you are keen on DIY, you might go to a DIY superstore and buy an electric drill. You would have to be a singularly sad individual to buy an electric drill for its own intrinsic merits. You would only buy an electric drill if you could gain a benefit from it. In this case, the benefit is the ability to drill holes. So the *feature* is that it is a *drill*, the *benefit* is that it *enables you to drill holes*.

Let us look at another example. You move on to the gardening department of that particular DIY superstore and purchase a lawn mower with a roller on the back of it. The feature of this mower is that it has a *roller*. What is the benefit? The answer is the roller *gives you stripes* on your lawn.

A further example might be purchasing a car. Two key features of this car are that it has *airbags* and *ABS* (Automatic Braking System). What is the benefit of these? Clearly, *safety* is a benefit, but it is not the selling benefit in the mind of the purchasing customer. What you are actually buying is *peace of mind.*

The phrase that links features and benefits and that helps you understand whether you are actually talking about a benefit or a feature is *which means.* A drill, which means holes; a roller mower, which means stripes; ABS braking and airbags, which means safety, which means peace of mind, which means . . .? There is no further benefit as such, so you have reached the ultimate benefit. By applying the "which means" test, you can ensure that you are offering your audience benefits.

Remember, the main difference between features and benefits is that whilst a feature will always *tell* you something about a product or service, it is the benefit that actually *sells* you on that product or service.

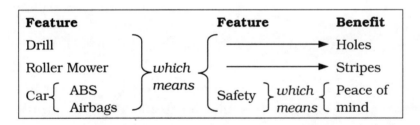

So we now understand that, generally speaking, people buy benefits and not features. However, remember that different audiences will have different perceptions of the benefit to them of the particular features of a product or service.

In the world of financial services, take the example of a bank's team of management buyout (MBO) specialists wanting to win the mandate from an owner-managed company. The owner wants to sell out to the rest of the management. The MBO team will naturally want to stress their efficiency in raising the necessary funds and also in continuing to support the bought-out management team, post-transaction. In short, the bank team will want to show that they will be committed both to the initial buyout transaction itself and also to the on-going relationship. This is a tough call.

It is to be expected that all but the most altruistic owner-managers and principal shareholders will be interested in extracting maximum shareholder value from the deal. In other words, they will want the management and new shareholders to pay as much as possible. This is completely against the interests of the existing management seeking the buyout. They will want a low valuation on the shares so they can demonstrate the maximum possible share value growth in the years to come as they develop the business through its next stages. This will be given added impetus no doubt by the existence of share options granted to the management at the time of the buyout deal. The faster the share value growth, the sooner the share options can kick in.

To allow the maximum headroom for future growth, the new management team will want to be sure that the bank they climb into bed with for the "one-night-stand" of the management buyout will in fact turn out to be a good lover in the medium term. Ideally they would like their new partner to develop into a loving and faithful spouse in the long term. For richer for poorer, in sickness and in health! The owner-manager, on the other hand, is more likely to be interested only in the one-night-stand, and a short but wild fling at the very most! Coming back down to earth, the owner-manager will be primarily interested in the short-term transactional abilities of the bank's MBO team, whilst the management will be primarily interested in building a long-term relationship with the bank.

So where does all this leave our bank's MBO team seeking to win the mandate? In financial institutions, there is often tension between the long-term relationship-building side and the short-term transactional element. In banking, you see this between, for example, the deal makers who often want to be quickly in and out of a situation, and the long-term relationship bankers who are keen to maintain hard-won friendships and trust between themselves and the bank's customers.

In accountancy, you see the same tension between tax advisers and auditors who often accuse their tax expert colleagues of damaging their long-term audit prospects by hitting clients with apparently heavy bills for tax advice. To cope with and square these competing tensions, you need to employ careful positioning, timing and adaptability. Essential here is to understand the concept of the *Decision Making Unit* or *DMU*. The DMU is made up of those people who will make the decision on the particular issue on which you are presenting. The numbers and seniority of people making up a DMU is directly proportional to the size of the proposed transaction in relation to the company's turnover.

With some decisions — the appointment of professional advisers, for example — the DMU will involve the majority if not all of the executive board of a company. However, making a decision to change the chilled water suppliers will normally involve fewer and more junior people.

Sometimes, there are subtle changes in the Decision Making Unit as the transaction progresses. Let us suppose you are a banker trying to win an MBO mandate. The DMU might change in shape and form from the initial presentational contact to later contacts with the prospect company. Initially, you might well be presenting to the company's executive team who may well have little shareholding in the venture. They will want the comfort of knowing that you would be good to work with, both during the highly stressful period of the buyout and beyond as the relationship develops post-buyout. They will be looking at your so-called "clubability" — your ability to get on with people and to strike up easy friendships. Fees and costs are not likely to be uppermost in their minds at this initial stage. Many presentations are made by MBO teams to managements for whom the buyout process is, at the time of presenting, very much in the future.

Once the prospect becomes a probability for a management buyout, the DMU will inevitably change to reflect the interest of the shareholders. They will be looking for the least-cost options from an MBO team keen to maximise shareholder value. Clearly, the approach will have to be different. The presenting team will have to shift the emphasis to take account of the new make-up of the DMU.

The Rule of Three and Lists

The Rule of Three is a very powerful oratorical device. It is used extensively by politicians and, wherever you can, try to plan these constructions into your presentation. It is based on the well-tried and tested storytelling method of postulating *three stages in the development of the narrative.* The most classic example of the rule of three is the standard joke about the Englishman, the Irishman and the Scotsman.

The principle translates best into spoken communications by producing a crescendo across the three points, with the final thrust being clearly on the third and last point; it can be represented graphically as follows:

Rule of Three

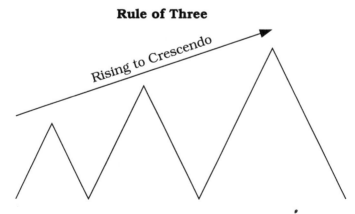

The key point to remember here is that, to be effective, the Rule of Three must be delivered with a crescendo leading to your third point punchline. If you put it across with flat delivery, you will lose the potential of the full impact.

The Rule of Three can also be used to deprecate as well as build up; in this case, you are actually diminishing the peaks in size as you go through the three points. A good example of this was General "Stormin' Norman" Schwarzkopf during the Gulf War when he described Saddam Hussein thus:

> "As a military leader he's no strategist, he's no tactician, but apart from that he's an OK guy."

Beware of overusing the Rule of Three, as it has become quite easy to spot, especially where the use is laboured. Before the landslide Labour victory in the 1997 British election, the actress Joanna Lumley, herself no slouch when it comes to the spoken word, famously warned on a pre-election TV chat show to "watch out for all those threes that the politicians will use".

Clearly they have not been chastened by Ms Lumley's words, because two years later they were still at it. In 1999, I witnessed a speech by William Hague, leader of the Conservative Party in Britain, who used at least 15 Rules of Three in a 35-minute presentation.

Lists are another method of creating impact through emphasis. A list should be at least five items long and again you can use it to create maximum passion if you add to your lists crescendos leading to the final item. It is helpful also in the performance to use your fingers to emphasise each item on your list. Here, though, it is a good idea to rehearse in front of a mirror so you can be sure your hands can be properly seen for maximum effect. All too often, speakers feel they are really socking it to the audience with terrific hand gestures, when in reality what they perceive to be extravagant hand movements are minuscule gestures, hardly discernible to the audience. I will expand on the whole issue of body language in Chapter 4.

We discussed in the previous chapter how, in the western world, the average attention span is just three and a quarter minutes. This means you must add variety to refresh your presentation and prevent your audience from getting bored. You do this through the use of crescendo, just as composers do when writing music. Make sure your speech has plenty of crescendos and, of course, at the very end, you need a powerful crescendo to leave the audience on a high note. To achieve effective crescendos, you will by definition have to plan parts of your presentation in a lower key. Do not worry that this will mean your speech will pack less punch in places. Effective communication relies on the changes in pitch and delivery to be truly effective in keeping the audience interested and attentive.

Mind your Language!

As we have discussed earlier, it is critical when making presentations to be very aware of what your audience is expecting to hear. Naturally this applies to content, but it also applies to the kind of language you use. We all use different language depending on our audiences and in some cases we fall into these different ways of speaking naturally. For example, when we talk to small children we use different language to that employed when we speak to our peers. Often men use some forms of words with other men that they would not dream of using with women. These natural linguistic inhibitions often need to be applied in a more studied fashion when it comes to business presentations.

The area of technical language is fraught with difficulties. All too frequently, technically qualified people tend to forget that their audience may not be as familiar with the forms of words which they themselves use in their everyday dealings. It is vital to use non-technical language to a non-technical audience. If you have to use technical language then you will have to explain it as you go along.

Jargon is fine where it serves as shorthand and where the audience will understand precisely what you mean. However, I have a very strict definition of jargon:

> *Jargon is a word or phrase that just one person*
> *in the audience does not understand.*

From that strict test, you will see that it is vital to explain jargonistic words if you feel there is a risk that there is just one person in the audience who might not know what you are talking about. There is a danger that in doing this you may appear to patronise members of the audience who do know what a particular piece of jargon means. Here you can obviate this by using softening phrases, which are discussed later.

The whole area of political correctness and sexism is one which spills over in our use of language. I still find when dealing with clients that a number of them use inappropriate language. For many, changing their use of language is quite a tough call. Many of them argue intellectually that it is as much a bias against them to insist that they change their language to fit in with what they see as new fads. Some would have great sympathy with such arguments and there is no doubt that on occasion political correctness can stretch the English language to almost farcical extremes. In local government throughout the English-speaking world, it is now considered correct in many councils to speak not of the "chairman" but of the "chair". Indeed, there was one example a few years back when councillors debated for over an hour what the correct term should be. Eventually, they decided by a narrow majority that the person hitherto referred to as chairman would henceforth be known as chair. At that point, someone who was in favour of the status quo got up and announced that he was no longer the "spokesman" but the "spoke" for his particular party!

Clearly, how far you take things is a matter for you and, indeed, the particular audience with which you are dealing. In the final analysis, you may wish to stand on your dignity, but you have a straight choice of either sticking to your principles or being effective in getting your message across to the audience. Obviously, sexist language is a different case in point and no one has a right through his or her language to make another person feel inferior. In the business world, very few people these days would dream of using racist language and there is no doubt that, in ten years' time, it is unlikely that sexist language will ever rear its head.

The final situation facing people grasping for appropriate language in their presentations is where the audience contains individuals who do not have English as a first language. Here, one has to remember that whilst such individuals may have a good command of the English language, they may not fully understand all the nuances of the more extreme idioms that might be employed. I remember being around one table when an Australian announced that the deal was so good that we should be able to "rip the arse out of it"! A number of puzzled eyebrows shot up at the imagery that he conjured up. It does not take too long to think up a whole host of English idioms and sayings which may tax some audiences: *a different kettle of fish*; *a silk purse out of a sow's ear* (watch this one in the Middle East); *falling between two stools* and so on.

Remember too that certain words have particular connotations. The hair care company, Clairol, once introduced a new design of curling tong known as a "Mist Stick" to the German market, only to find out that this would not have had universal appeal to the average German female. Similarly, Rolls Royce only just renamed a car for a German market in the nick of time that had hitherto in the UK been known as the Silver Mist.

Similarly, the innocent use of a phrase such as "this might be our cue to advance our cause", might bring some mirth to a French audience as *Cue* is the name of a notorious porno-graphic magazine!

Inevitably you can never be totally sure that a word used innocently in English will not give you problems when trans-lated elsewhere but the key is to ensure that you keep things as simple as possible for non-mother-tongue English speak-ers.

Forms of Words

There are a number of forms of words which will help you out of potentially difficult situations. Some are frequently used across the board in everyday presentations. Others tend to be for rather more specialised presentation environments — the announcement of redundancies, for example.

Below are a number of useful words and phrases which can work well if judiciously applied to spoken communications. Remember, however, that wherever possible being straightfor-ward and honest with your audience always pays off in the long run. Your utterances will get you nowhere if they are re-garded as "weasel words". If all else fails, try honesty — it may just get you out of a jam!

Softening phrases

Use softening words and phrases where you want to reduce the risk of being perceived as know-all or arrogant. They are helpful if you are presenting to audiences older or more senior in position to yourself. It is important to get this right and not overuse them; otherwise you run the risk of appearing rather too unctuous and eager to please. These phrases are at their most useful when you are dealing with audiences with mixed levels of knowledge about a given subject. Here you can use concepts and jargon which may be new to some elements of the audience without appearing to patronise those who already know what you are talking about.

> "As you will know . . ."
>
> "As you may be aware . . ."
>
> "You won't need me to tell you . . ."
>
> "You'll need no reminding . . ."
>
> "You will no doubt remember . . ."

Note how the word *you* is used in all of the above phrases. Such phrasing takes advantage of the fact that in the English language the word *you* is the same in both singular and plural. Remember, you are seeking to influence your audience as individuals no matter how many individuals you happen to be talking to at any one time. A common trap many presenters fall into is to insert the word *all* into phrases such as those above, thus rendering the use of the word *you* unambiguously in the plural form and thus removing the intimacy of the singular *you*. Thus:

> "We should be able to fund this project on a DCF basis, which as you will know, means that we will use Discounted Cash Flow as the basis of our analysis."

Words which Get You Out of a Jam

There will inevitably be occasions when you will find yourself in a corner and under pressure. This can be especially the case if you are in a senior position and find yourself having to answer difficult questions either to disgruntled staff who have heightened expectations of what you can tell them about a difficult business situation or to the media who are just curious and keen to turn over stones. Often question-and-answer sessions can throw up the most unexpected of requests for information. The first rule of answering such questions is *don't flannel.* There is no God-given rule that you have to be omniscient. If you do not know the answer, then say so.

Sometimes you will know the answer but prefer not to give it because as that particular time it will be unhelpful either for legal reasons, for reasons of confidentiality or that it will jeopardise the company's interests at the that particular time. Here a great word to lean on is *appropriate.* Thus:

> "I cannot give you the answer to that question because it is not appropriate at this time . . . for legal reasons . . . because of confidentiality . . . because now is not the appropriate time to discuss such matters in depth."

> "I would very much like to answer your questions in full but I hope you will understand that it would not be appropriate for me to talk about these matters at this difficult time . . ."

Note how in the last example we are using another phrase which is aimed at getting the sympathy of the audience:

> "I hope you will understand . . ."

Try too its variant:

> "I hope you will appreciate . . ."

The word *appropriate* can be used to be rather more specific about a given situation. Take job losses, for example. Inevitably, when conveying news of redundancies to both internal and external audiences, you will be asked whether there will be any more job losses. No modern organisation can rule out absolutely future job losses but understandably you will not at such a sensitive time want to make such a bald statement. Instead, use the word *appropriate.*

> "Any modern forward-thinking organisation will always want to have a workforce which is appropriate to its needs both in terms of numbers and skill set. There will always be adjustments in terms of numbers both up and down, so we may find ourselves employing more people in future."

Many managers have learned that it is possible to use such potentially difficult situations to restate their policy on job losses thus:

> "Wherever possible, we aim to achieve reductions in numbers through retraining and job shifting followed by voluntary job packages. We regard redundancy as the last step in a managed plan to ensure we have a workforce appropriate to our needs, and only then as a last resort."

Another good word to employ where at a given point in time you find yourself unable to give the full story is *current*. Thus:

> "We have no current plans for more redundancies."

This phrase might be used where you have made one set of cuts at, say, a particular operating unit but are still investigating whether further job losses are necessary at other locations. Beware of overusing this word, as it has become seen by many as code for, "We think there will need to be more cuts but we are not prepared to announce them yet." Such interpretations can only serve to heighten feelings of unease and do nothing to enhance relations between workforce and management. Remember that honesty is the best policy. Try your best to be as candid as circumstances allow, but if you have to be guarded in your remarks, try to use a time frame as a context for what you have to say. Thus:

> "You will appreciate that these are difficult times for the industry as a whole. We cannot therefore at this stage rule out further job losses but neither are they

> definitely ruled in. We should have a better picture in a
> month or two once we have seen the latest government
> figures on . . ."

You could then go on to reconfirm your organisation's enlightened policy on job losses and redundancy.

"No Comment" is No Comment

One of the worst phrases anyone in a position of authority can
use is "No comment". It is widely regarded as the refuge of the
guilty who has everything to hide. So what can you say instead when a questioner has clearly put their finger on a delicate situation to which you know the answer but which you
are not prepared to discuss or disclose at that time. Sometimes questioners hang themselves by introducing phrases
such as:

> "There's been speculation that . . ."

or

> "There are reports that . . ."

It is easy to dismiss the first with:

> "I hope you will understand that in our position we can
> only deal with facts and not speculation . . ."

The second assertion can be dealt with by:

> "I have not seen these reports and I hope you will agree
> with me that it would not therefore be appropriate to
> discuss them."

Of course you can only say that if you genuinely have not seen
such reports. If you have seen the reports, try:

> "I have seen these reports but they do not tell the full
> story [inevitably reports will not be as full as your
> knowledge of the situation] — suffice to say . . ."

Back to "No comment". Far better when confronted with a question to which you do not wish to give a definitive answer to say:

> "I am sorry, I would like to be helpful but I can neither confirm nor deny that . . ."

which is along similar lines to:

> "This can neither be ruled in or ruled out . . ."

If pressed for more elucidation, a good technique is to throw yourself on the mercy of the audience:

> "I would like to help you but, forgive me — I hope you will appreciate that I can say no more on this at this time . . ."

The Call to Action

How many times have you listened to a presentation and asked yourself: "Well, that's all very well, but what am I supposed to do?" So many presentations leave the audience puzzled as to what their next step should be. Remember our definition of a successful communication:

> "One which modifies the behaviour of the audience so
> that they do something in your favour that they would
> not have done had you not spoken to them."

If you have planned your presentations successfully, taking into account your analysis of the audience, you must have a clear idea of what it is you expect them to do. What is more, you must tell them — clearly and specifically. Do not leave it to chance in the hope that somehow they will have picked up the gist of what it is you want them to do. We call this the *call to action*. The call to action can be something very obvious like winning the business you are pitching for or a sales team going out and delivering or exceeding its targets. Often, the call to action relates to some time in the future, such as people taking on board some information which they feel empowers them to make use of it at a later stage when a suitable opportunity arises. Either way, there needs to be a clear call to action planned in to your content.

Clearly, getting the content right is a key step in any presentation. Many people believe that content is all. Others feel that style of delivery is more important. The truth is, they are both essential elements of any successful presentation, but only once you are sure that you have got the content right are you ready to move closer to the hour of the presentation itself.

Key Points to Remember

- Don't construct your presentation as you would a written report. It will come across as turgid and boring.

- Use headlines to grab your audience's attention.

- Ask yourself, "What will really make the audience sit up and listen?"

- People buy benefits, not features. Emphasise the benefits of your product or message.

- Use the Rule of Three and Lists to emphasise particular points.

- Choose your words carefully if you are dealing with a delicate situation.

- Always finish with a clear call to action.

Chapter 3

THEORY INTO PRACTICE (2): PREPARATION AND VISUAL AIDS

According to a survey carried out by The Aziz Corporation, 76 per cent of all people in business believe that making a presentation in public is the most daunting task they have to do in the world of commerce. It is not surprising then that when people are faced with the prospect of a presentation, their first reaction is invariably panic. This feeling of panic is soon followed by the shelving of the presentation because, strangely, other things become a priority. A few days later, the prospect of the presentation looms again. Again more panic and, if there is time, the project is shelved once more. This probably goes on until just a couple of days before the presentation is due to be given. Then the panic is immense. Often, the individual's whole department is thrown into a flurry as people are dispatched to create visual aids, find information and all the decks are cleared in order to get the presentation prepared. It is a highly tense, pressurised process resulting in the individual becoming stressed to the nth degree.

Eventually, the presentation is given. Congratulations are offered and the presenter leaves the presentation knowing that yet again they "got away with it". (Incidentally, you will invariably be praised rather than criticised for a presentation, firstly because most people sympathise with your plight and secondly they usually don't know how to make a presentation themselves and certainly have no way in which they can con-structively criticise anybody else's presentation.)

And so it goes on; there is nothing like the prospect of a presentation to create a cycle of despair in an individual. The starting point for an effective presentation must therefore be preparation, and that preparation must be timely and it must be adequate. Of course, most people say they haven't enough time to make presentations. In my view, presentations are rather like marriage: if they are entered into in haste, you have a whole lifetime during which you can regret your rashness. I very much believe in the application of the six P's principle in presentation, which goes like this:

Pathetically poor preparation leads to
pathetically poor presentation

The first stage of any preparation is to ask the key questions we learned in Chapter 1. Here they are again:

- Who is the audience?

- What do they want to hear?

- What do I want to say?

- Where is the overlap?

This is where your preparation starts. These key questions must be asked as soon as you receive the request to present.

An important element of your preparation is consultation. Here it is vital that you do not rely on your own view of what the audience will want, but seek the views of others who might give another perspective of what they are looking for. This is particularly true if you are making a presentation to an exter-nal audience.

Consultation is also useful when it comes to finding out just how much the audience can be expected to know on a given subject. Here is another golden rule:

Never underestimate the intelligence of the audience,
but do not overestimate their knowledge

To Script or Not To Script?

We are often asked whether writing a script is the best way forward for a presentation. The answer to that is usually no. The reason is that most people are not trained to write an effective script for speaking. Again, most of our education has been focused on the written word and in fact we speak very differently to the way that we have been taught to write. The effect of trying to read out loud something that has been written in what we call "print speak" is usually very stilted and boring. It is much better to make notes first and then reduce these to bullet points. You can then use these bullet points to make your speech.

Even speech writers are often tested when it comes to writing a speech for someone else. It is a very good speech writer indeed who can write in a style which a particular speaker finds comfortable. However, if you do wish to have a full script (some people need this for political or commercial reasons), then the chart below shows how to create a spoken script with the least difficulty and without the need of a speech writer.

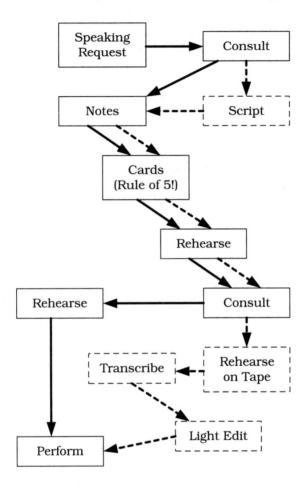

To understand how the chart works, let us go through it stage by stage. Firstly, you might write out in your own way — essentially using *print speak* — what it is you want to say. You should then boil this speech down to bullet points which you will put on cards, usually 6"x4" (5"x3" cards are more discrete for after-dinner speaking). You then rehearse what it is you want to say using those cards and then rehearse on tape using a dictating machine. Then have the tape transcribed. When you do, you will be horrified at how ungrammatically you speak. Don't worry about this; this is exactly how we normally do speak and, more importantly, it is how the audience is expecting to hear you. It is important, therefore, that in editing the transcript you do not put back all the print speak constructions; simply edit for factual correctness. The script that you are then left with is one that you can speak effectively, because it will be in your own spoken words.

I should emphasise that, when it comes to effectiveness, reading from a script, even one prepared in the way outlined above, is usually less successful than reading from bullet points on cards. In the majority of speaking situations, you should opt for speaking off cards using the Rule of Five. The Rule of Five is very simple. It says that each card has no more than five lines per card and no more than five words per line. You should write in pencil and in block capitals so that you can easily read what you have written and instead of crossing out you can erase and rewrite where changes are necessary. This way, your eyes will not be overloaded when they try to read your notes.

> - *RULE OF FIVE*
> - *BULLET POINTS*
> - *LARGE CAPS IN PENCIL*
> - *< FIVE WORDS PER LINE*
> - *< FIVE LINES PER CARD*

Work on the principle of having one card for each one minute of speech. If you do this and you are obeying the Rule of Five, you simply have to find six words for every one word on your bullet points. Soon, as you become more capable and used to the methodology, you will find that you can make a speech using one card to prompt you for two minutes. Good speakers use just one card and can make a half-hour presentation from that card which they usually do not refer to at all. All it requires is practice and dedication to the methodology.

Rehearsal Is Key

Great actors like, say, Kenneth Branagh or Emma Thompson do not respectively leap onto the stage of the RSC and begin a performance of *King Lear* or sashay onto a film set without first having picked up the play or script, learned the lines and rehearsed. Arguably, great actors have more talent than the average businessperson in the area of spoken communication, so if they have to rehearse, surely you should? Time spent on rehearsal pays great dividends. A rehearsal of a ten-minute presentation should take just that — ten minutes. If it takes longer, then the chances are your presentation is longer than you thought.

There is a great temptation when going through rehearsals to delude yourself about the overall timing of a presentation based on how long it takes you to "flick through the cards". Don't be fooled; so many presentations have foundered because people have not realised how much they are over-running and it is very easy indeed to lose all track of time when you are making a presentation. Another phenomenon to bear in mind is the tendency, despite rehearsal, for the presentation itself to run longer when you go "live". Speakers should build in a ten per cent under-run as a contingency. So, if you're aiming for a ten-minute presentation, plan for nine; if 20 minutes, plan for 18, and so on. Remember: you are more likely to be forgiven for under-running than over-running!

You should aim to do at least two full rehearsals of presentation and you should, if possible, rehearse in front of someone. They will give you valuable feedback, for example, about jokes. The definition of a joke is something that makes people laugh, instantly. If you have to explain the joke, then clearly it's not going to work on the day. Remember too that the joke that sounded great in the bar at 10.30 at night does not always go down so well at 9.30 the following morning in the cold light of day. The rule for jokes is:

If in doubt, cut them out

Wherever possible, rehearse in front of someone who is typical of the audience that you will be addressing. One of our clients who is very senior is particularly adept at following our advice and finding individuals in his organisation who can do just this. Encourage them to give you open and honest feedback. Only in this way can your presentation improve.

It goes without saying that you should ensure that you have some kind of rehearsal at the venue itself. Often, it is not possible to have a full rehearsal, particularly if you are speaking for 40 minutes, an hour, or even longer. By the time you arrive at the venue, you should already be well enough rehearsed in the words offsite. What you must have is what is known as a technical run-through or "stagger through". This is where you work along with the technical operator to ensure that all the various cues for slide changes, demonstrations, etc. work and are understood by the technician. Inevitably, the more complicated the presentation, the more you will need some kind of script if you are to be absolutely certain the technician is to change the slides at the right time (see "Visual Aids" below). There may well also be lighting changes that have to be brought about and there may be a sound technician who has to cue in music or effects and ensure that the correct microphones are faded up. Whatever the level of sophistication, you will need at least some kind of running order and possibly a full script. Refer to the methodology given earlier to arrive at a script in a trouble-free way with the least effort, but nonetheless a script which you can speak effectively and with passion.

A final word on rehearsals. They really are essential. This is especially true where you are doing complex demonstrations. Years ago, I remember appearing on the BBC children's television programme *Blue Peter*. I was to demonstrate how to cook the perfect curry. The editor of the programme, which went out live at 5.00 p.m. twice a week, insisted that we assembled at 9.00 a.m. with enough ingredients and utensils to do five — yes, five — full rehearsals. That meant cooking five curries. This applied to every item in the programme. The effect, although tedious by way of rehearsal, was to ensure that nothing went wrong when we finally did it for real. The live performance went like a dream, although by the end of the day even the most ardent fan of Indian food was thoroughly sick of the thought of more curry!

Visual Aids

Visual aids, by definition, should be *visual* and they should be *aids to the audience* and not crutches for you. Today, there is a wealth of visual aids and visual aid media that we can use. The trick is to use only as much as is necessary and no more. Too often, we see presenters hiding behind the technology of their visual aids. This effectively excludes the best visual aid that they have — *themselves*.

Another all-too-common phenomenon is "visual aids" that are nothing more than the speaker's notes up on the screen masquerading as visual aids. They serve only to help them lurch from one subject to the next.

Inevitably, visual aids will often be textual in nature. Here we need to follow a number of rules in order to make our textual visual aids effective. The first is to remember that you are seeking to support what it is you are saying rather than offer the audience huge tracts of text, which can only serve to divert them from listening to what you are saying. So the KISS principle comes into play:

KISS stands for Keep It Simple, Stupid.

In practice, this means that we must not overload the slides/acetates with vast amounts of text. Again, we apply the Rule of Five. The rule is drawn directly from the world of television graphics, where they discovered very early on that this tended to be the most easily understood way of presenting textual information on the screen. No more than five lines per slide and no more than five words per line. Note that this is a maximum, and it is often possible to be effective with far fewer words on any given slide.

Many people struggle with boiling down their words to fit onto a slide to obey the ruthless dictates of the Rule of Five. To do this, it is worth remembering what I have come to call the *Fresh Fish Rule*. This was first taught me by a Glaswegian sub-editor when many, many years ago I was a down-table sub-editor at BBC Broadcasting House in London. He told me of a sign which exists to this day on a shop wall in the village of Stockbridge in Hampshire. The sign simply says *"Fresh Fish Sold Here"*. He asked me what was wrong with that sign. I replied, "Nothing". He insisted it was too long and asked me which was the most redundant word that could be removed without changing the sign's impact. The answer, of course, was *"Here"*. After all, who puts a sign up unless they are selling something at that particular location?

He then asked for the next most redundant word, which was *"Sold"* — not many people go to the trouble of creating a sign unless they are actually selling something. The next most redundant word is *"Fresh"*, because it's a given that you're not selling rotten fish. Well I got all of this right, but my Glaswegian sub-editor was not satisfied. He said "You dunna need *fush*, 'cuz you can smell it half a mile away!"

The Fresh Fish rule serves to illustrate how words can be reduced, but in this particular instance, much better than words would have been a *picture* of a fish.

When applying "Fresh Fish" to textual slides, the key thing is to look at what you have written and knock out all the inefficient words. Usually these are small words such as *a, an, the* etc. Another rule of thumb is that if the text is grammatical, then your slide is probably over-written. Make use of plus and minus signs to indicate increases and decrease, or where possible up and down arrows. For example, a slide which says:

Sales up by more than 100 per cent

could be better written as:

Sales ↑ 100%

There are occasions where you do use grammatical text and these are normally where you are using a direct quote or, for example, a mission statement. In these circumstances, it is helpful to insert the text in quotation marks, thus:

> "Our mission is to add value to your business by helping your people become more effective communicators"

Visual Aid Media

You will usually have to opt for some way of presenting your visual aids. Which you choose may often be driven by what is available and, if you are making an external presentation, the equipment available at the venue. Size of audience is an important factor too. Some visual aid media have been with us for some time. Others, such as computer graphics, have yet to become universal in their use.

35mm Slides

35mm slides are still widely used and have the advantage of providing, if designed correctly, a highly professional image for the presentation. When using 35mm slides, or indeed any visual aid where a darkened room is required, it is always better to have brighter text out of a darker background. Avoid colours that strain the eyes such as red and always ensure that you have good contrast between the colour choices.

Increasingly, people are using personal computers to design their slides, handing a computer disk to a slide production bureau to turn out the slides themselves. Sometimes results can be disappointing because whilst slides appear legible on the computer screen, they do not translate well onto slide. This is a result of two factors. First, the resolution of a computer screen is usually superior; and second, slides are viewed on the computer from a distance of no more than couple of feet, whereas the distance of the viewer from a projected slide screen can be several feet.

35mm slides have for several years been the traditional visual aid and certainly still have a significant place in many presentations. 35mm slide projectors are almost universally present in the business environment.

They are particularly valuable in large formal environments, as they can be projected onto large screens with no loss of colour density and therefore they retain their impact. They provide an opportunity, when correctly designed, of producing a highly professional visual image that can only serve to enhance the effectiveness of the presentation. Ensure your slides carry "branding" in, say, the form of a logo at the bottom right hand corner of each slide.

The disadvantage of 35mm slides is that they tend to be inflexible in as much as you usually have to settle on the content of your slides well in advance of the presentation. This means being especially careful to check facts and figures. I was once asked at the eleventh hour to coach a team of presenters only to discover that they had to scrap half of the 64 expensively produced 35mm slides because they contained misspellings or were factually incorrect. By the time you get to within 24 hours of the presentation, there is very little scope for making any changes other than dropping a slide that is incorrect.

There are a number of tips worth bearing in mind when using 35mm slides. Firstly, always insist that your slides are glass-mounted. These days, most reputable graphics organisations and slide production bureaux do this as a matter of course. Glass-mounting the slides ensures that you avoid image distortion caused by the buckling of the film under the heat of the projector lamp.

A disadvantage of glass mounting can be the so-called "Newton's rings" effect that occurs when two transparent surfaces are pressed close together. This is a rainbow-like halo that can be distracting in certain circumstances. However, as long as the slides have been mounted in clean conditions, this ought to be avoided.

Both 35mm slides and slide projectors can suffer from condensation if they are brought from a cold environment such as the boot of a car to the warm environment of a presentation room or conference hall. This condensation can result in unsightly blobs appearing on the slides, which then proceed to change their shape as they disappear with the warming up of the slide. Often, audiences find this more interesting than the presentation itself! To minimise this risk, carry both slides and projector in the passenger compartment of your car and try to bring your slides into the warm environment a good hour before the presentation is due to take place.

Cleanliness is vital with 35mm slides. There is nothing worse than viewing a grubby slide, particularly if the background is light in colour. Always carry a soft cloth — if possible a spectacle-cleaning cloth — with you and give your slides a final polish before your presentation.

Most slide projectors in business use either a linear or carousel magazine to hold your slides. The latter is most popular in the business context, as it allows you to load up to 80 slides into one cassette.

When using slides for external presentation, ensure that you find out whether they will be *front-projected* (that is, with the projector throwing the image onto the screen from the back of the hall), or *back-projected* (where the projector is hidden behind or to the side of the screen). This will have a bearing on how you load your slides. Slides should be loaded by standing to one side of the projector and looking at the screen. When loading for front projection, the slides should appear to you as you look at the screen to be legible (that is, the writing the right way round) and upside down. When back-projected, the slides should appear, as you look at the screen from the back, the "wrong" way round (that is, a mirror image) and upside down. If the back projection system is one where the projector is at the side and a 45-degree mirror is used to save space, then the slides should be inserted as you would for front projection. It goes without saying that you should always check each slide before any presentation. We have all witnessed the mess presenters get into when they discover a slide is upside down and then try to sort it out.

One final tip: the length of time a slide is up on a screen during a presentation can vary enormously. Quite often, you will want to talk about a subject that is not illustrated by a particular slide. Rather than have the previous slide stay up until your next slide change, invest in a number of either blank slides or generic slides with, for example, the logo of your company or the mission statement. These can be inserted at key points where required so that you can talk without necessarily having to relate to a particular slide on the screen.

Overhead Projector Slides (OHPs)

Overhead projector slides or view foils, otherwise know as acetates, are another common presentation visual aid. They have been around since the early 1950s and were almost universal in business presentations, particularly internal ones, during the 1960s and 1970s. Indeed, internal presentations in certain companies were never considered complete without an armful of view foils. As a visual aid, they have tended to be abused and misused over the years and many is the audience that has inwardly groaned at the sight of a presenter arriving on stage armed with a huge stack of foils. However, used effectively, overhead projector slides can be one of the most powerful forms of visual aid. Wherever possible, they should be printed in colour and of course should obey the Rule of Five and the Fresh Fish Rule. As with 35mm slides, branding in the bottom right hand corner should be the norm and again, as with 35mm slides, cleanliness is vital. Many people make the mistake of printing small black text onto each acetate. This projects with acres of white space around the text and comes across as dull and uninteresting. Try to use a colour printer wherever possible and make the text as large as possible without it looking ridiculous. If you do not have access to a colour printer, then you should use special acetate pens to "colour up" your foils.

It is critical to ensure that the slides are correctly positioned on the top of the overhead projector. You may wish to consider using cardboard mounts for your slides, which make them easier to handle. Cardboard mounts also make it easier to ensure that the slides are correctly positioned on the OHP. Most modern overhead projectors have two sets of locating lugs that fit into the slide mount. This ensures that as long as your projector is correctly aligned, the slides will always be level and even.

Slide management is critical if you are not to get into a tangle during your presentations, as OHPs can be unwieldy and cumbersome to handle. If you are not using cardboard mounts, ensure that your slides are spread out in a fan-like pattern on the desk in front of you with the first slide uppermost. This will help you manage the slides on to the OHP and then off again to the other side of the OHP, thus avoiding confusion of used slides with slides that have yet to be shown.

Some OHP acetates are printed with a paper backing. This should be removed before the presentation begins. There is nothing more annoying that the sound of paper being rent from an acetate as you proceed through your presentation.

Setting Up the OHP

Most overhead projectors are designed to project a square image onto a screen. However, because of the nature of the projection system, which uses a lens and a mirror, if you project onto a screen that is hanging vertically, you will end up with a trapezoid projected image. This is known as the keystone effect. It can be overcome by tilting the top of the screen forwards to compensate for the distortion in the projection throw. Most modern screens have a ratcheted arm at the top to enable you to do this. You need to experiment with the degree of screen angle to obtain optimum results. The image should appear square when viewed from the front. Needless to say, this should be done before the audience arrives!

The next thing to check is the fringing control. Again, because of the nature of the overhead projection system, if this is not properly adjusted, you end up with an orange or rainbow-like halo around the image. This can be adjusted through moving either a lever or a knob, usually on the lower part of the projector, until the fringing disappears. Obviously, your projected image has to be in focus and this is usually achieved by adjusting a gnarled knob, which moves the lens and mirror assembly above the OHP up and down, until you get a crisp image. Remember, it is the distance of the OHP from the screen that will determine the size of the image and you should try to ensure that the top edge of the image is aligned with the top edge of the screen. The higher the image on the screen, the easier it will be for your audience to see it. You may find that your image does not line up exactly with the screen itself; in this instance, try to ensure that at least one edge is aligned with one edge of the screen by twisting the OHP until it does.

A question frequently asked about the use of overhead projectors is, "Should you leave them on all the time or switch them on and off in between slide changes?" Our advice is to have the first slide ready on the top of the OHP with the projector switched off. Switch this slide on when you are ready to talk about it. In many presentations, however, the first slide is (and we would advise this) a generic slide showing the title of the presentation and the presenter's name and title. It is important to remind people who you are, particularly if you have a name with an unusual spelling or one that could be misheard. In large organisations, presenters often wrongly assume that internal audiences are bound to know you. Don't bank on this. It does no harm at all to spell it out on the title slide. Do not be shy about this; you really do need to remind people who you are.

Although there is a disadvantage in having white light projected as you change slides, we would advise leaving the projector on throughout the performance. This is because switching an OHP on and off greatly increases the chance of the bulb blowing. Although most modern projectors have a spare bulb which can easily be switched over to, it can still be very disconcerting to have a bulb blow during a presentation. Also, Sod's Law says that the standby bulb will itself probably have been blown during a previous presentation! However, if there are going to be periods of time when the slide on show will not be relevant, then of course you can switch the overhead projector off until you are ready to move on. Another possibility is to have a slide containing a mission statement or some key overriding principle projected during sections of your presentation when you are not otherwise using the OHP. This not only solves the problem, it also serves to remind the audience of the philosophy behind your speech.

Where should you stand? Well, the key here is to make life easy for yourself. If you talk to actors, they will tell you that doing what they call any kind of "business" — that is, the manipulation of props or pieces of paper or, in this case, view foils — calls for greater powers of concentration and it is terribly easy to get confused. You can make it much easier for yourself by organising things so that, if you are right-handed, you stand to the left of the projector. By doing this, your right hand can be used to lift slides on and off the projector, Similarly, if you are left-handed, you stand to the right of the machine. It is important of course to organise things so that you are not obscuring the screen from any major part of the audience.

Most people do not make best use of the OHP's unique facility that allows you to write on the slide during the presentation. Many successful presentations are made through preparing slides which are incomplete, so you can fill in certain key figures or directional arrows with felt tip pen live during the presentation (ensure that they are special marker pens for overhead foils, as not all pens work effectively on acetate). Even if you have to do a series of presentations using the same view foils, through using water-based pens, you can effect this technique and then clean the slides afterwards with a little dampened tissue. Again, if you are standing with your writing hand closest to the machine, this makes life a lot easier.

Another facility the overhead projector system allows you is the ability to create overlapped slides. This can be most effective in, for example, building up graphs. By using sticky tape, you can fold over several elements of foil onto a base foil to build up a picture in a most effective way.

One of the most annoying aspects of overhead projector foils from an audience's point of view is the use of the so-called "reveal" on a slide. This is where the presenter places a slide onto the overhead projector and then immediately covers up half of it with a piece of paper in the belief that the audience of course has seen nothing of what is underneath. Invariably, they do and this only serves to confuse and annoy. A much more effective way of achieving these reveals is to use

"Post-It" notes, which can be stuck over the top of the text you wish to reveal. As an *aide memoire,* you can write on the top of the Post-Its the information that lies below; in this way, you will not be surprised by what you reveal!

When overhead projector slides are used to their greatest effect, they can be most powerful. However, there is one over-riding sin that many presenters perpetrate, particularly with OHPs: looking at the screen. There is absolutely no need to look at the overhead projector screen itself, because what you see on the top of the OHP looking directly at the foil is exactly what your audience will see when looking at the screen. If the slide is back-to-front or upside down, that is how it will appear on the screen itself. There is no need, once you have set up your projector correctly, to ever look at the screen. The effect of looking at the screen is to detract firstly from your own presentation, because what you are doing is inviting the audience to look at the screen and not you. Nobody was ever persuaded by a screen. Secondly, the act of turning your back on the audience will mean that many of them will not be able to follow your words. So the golden rule is:

Do not look at the screen!

Computer Generation

It was not until the mid-1990s that computer-generated slide presentations began to take off. Now we are able to create with our personal computers an immense range of visual effects. There are several software programmes that enable one to create professional-looking slides in a relatively short period of time. The most popular are PowerPoint, Lotus Freelance and Corel, and they all work on broadly similar lines. Of these, the Microsoft product PowerPoint is the market leader and my advice would be that if you are contemplating a computer generation software package, then you will not go far wrong by using PowerPoint.

However, there are a number of points that need to borne in mind. The first is the early versions of PowerPoint have to be translated by later versions of PowerPoint and often in the translation, some of the elements that make up your slide can become distorted, particularly symbols or bullet points. If you are making a PowerPoint presentation using someone else's equipment — for example, in a modern conference centre — you need to find out in advance what version of the software they are using. If it is a later version than yours, make sure well in advance that the translation is done so that you can adjust for any distortion that may have taken place. Similarly, there may be occasions whereby you have a later version than the equipment on which you are going to be making the presentation. This is trickier, as earlier versions are usually unable to read later versions and you may have to recreate or translate your later version in the earlier version software.

This is all beginning to sound a bit complicated, so here is a good watchword. For most senior managers, it is probably not worth you becoming terribly involved with the mechanics of the PowerPoint itself, except to know how to make last minute changes to your slides. It is much better strategically to identify within your department a younger person who will be more computer literate and more importantly who will not be as costly in terms of their "hourly rate" as you. In this way, you can get them to organise your PowerPoint presentations under your direction. This is a much better route forward than spending a great deal of your valuable time at your computer screen. Inevitably, you will not be able to put in the required time and the quality of your presentation will suffer. However, if you act as editor of the presentation, you will be able to ensure that this kind of input creates superior slides.

Presentational packages like PowerPoint offer you many more facilities than you really need to use in an effective presentation. Here again, the KISS principle must be applied rigorously. It is critical that you do not make your PowerPoint presentations over-busy; certainly, they should not look "gimmicky". Certain transitions — that is, the changes from one slide to the next — may look effective on a computer screen. However, they often do not look so good when they are transferred either to a television monitor through a *scan converter* (of which more later) or projected onto a larger screen using a data projector. Much of this is down to personal preference but transitions that I have found to be particularly irksome are the *venetian blind* effect, particularly in the vertical mode and also the *mosaic* dissolve effect.

Computer presentation software packages enable you to build your slides line-by-line — what they call *build effect*. This can be very useful, as it overcomes the tendency of the audience to read the fourth line of a particular slide when you are talking about the first line. One popular transition effect is to *fly each line in*. As we read from left to right in English, it is much better to fly each line in from the right rather than from the left. In this way, the audience can start to read the line as soon as it starts to fly in.

As the slide builds, you may wish to take advantage of the *grey out* facility; again, this is useful when building a slide to keep the audience's concentration on the line that you are talking about at any particular point.

Point size (the size of the type) is critical in computer-generated packages, as it is in any textual/visual aid. However, because of the greater resolution of a normal computer screen, it is easy to convince yourself that something is legible because you are viewing from a distance of half a metre from the computer screen. But the larger the audience, the further they will be from the screen.

In PowerPoint, for example, Microsoft recommend that you use a point size of no less than 18. I would advise that you should go for no less than 24 points for your text. This is a minimum and you should make the text as large as possible, commensurate with the slide not looking awkward or out of place. There is no need to ensure consistency of point size between slides; each slide must stand on its own merits.

The *font* or *type face* is also critical when creating textual slides. As with 35mm slides, sans serif fonts are the ones you should go for. Serifs are the names given to the little curlicues at the ends of letters in certain types of font. A font where the letters do not have these additions is known as sans serif, or without serifs. One of the most popular sans serif fonts is Arial. This is the font used throughout the world on road signs as it is the one that is most easily read from a distance. It tends to get overused in presentations as it is one of the first to appear in the list of fonts available in a presentation software package. There are, however, others that you could make use of. Try AvantGarde, Eurostile, Gill Sans or Helvetica as alternatives. The only time when you might consider using serif fonts is when you are putting up a quote or, indeed, using a corporate house-style to illustrate a particular point.

The importance of ensuring that slides can be properly read cannot be over-stressed. There are two basic ages of sensory senility that affect all human beings. The first is age 12, when hearing is most acute and starts to fall off, albeit very gradually, from that point. The second is around age 45. This is the point at which people who have not had to wear glasses to date find themselves needing glasses for close work. Invariably in the audiences to which you will be presenting, there will be people whose eyesight is not 20/20 vision. There is nothing more frustrating for people than to discover that they cannot read your slides. Indeed, I heard of one instance where a team of presenters pitching for business were asked to leave because of the frustration the main board had in reading their slides.

Props

Props tend to be forgotten in most business presentations. However, they can be an incredibly powerful way of making a point. A prop is the theatrical name given to any object that is used by an actor. In business terms, it can be, for example, a simple document, perhaps a report, which is held up and shown to the audience. However, when showing something to the audience, it is important to favour the audience's point of view. All too often, people will pick up a report and wave it in the air rather dismissively whilst at the same time saying how important the content of the report is.

It is vital that you give any object that you show due respect and importance. You may recall the old television adverts selling soap powder. Here the actor promoting the detergent would ensure that the box of powder was held very close to his face and square on to the audience where they can see it clearly. The key is to associate the box with the presenter's face. When showing a report, it is critical that the same technique is used.

Similarly, objects can be used to great effect. Some years ago, a client came to us from an insurance company which had lost a great deal of business to the then newly launched telephone insurance company Direct Line. Our client had to stand up in front of 600 of his top managers and emphasise to them that they were going to win back their market share from Direct Line. Instead of simply saying that, we persuaded him to pull out from behind the lectern, at just the right time, a bright red telephone with black wheels, which was the symbol of Direct Line, and kick it across the stage. Meanwhile, we played in the Direct Line theme, with a great distortion at the end of it. It brought the house down.

Props can be devastating, and in some cases, show-stoppers. Some years ago I was interviewing, live on a six o'clock television programme, the governor of a prison where a riot was taking place. It had been alleged that the cause of the riot was brutality by the prison officers against the inmates. After much pressing on this point, the governor, clearly irritated by my line of questioning, reached into his jacket pocket and pulled out a handkerchief. He held the handkerchief very still so that the close-up camera could get a shot of it. He peeled back the handkerchief to reveal what looked to be an ordinary bar of soap. "There you are, Mr Aziz — an ordinary bar of soap. But look more closely. In it are embedded fourteen razor blades. That was left in the prison officers' washroom. Who is brutalising whom in this prison?" Such a devastating prop was more effective than thousands of words.

Now, whilst you might not have use of bars of soap with razor blades embedded in them, there may well be objects and documents that you can use to enhance the effectiveness of your presentation. A word of warning here, however: if you talk to actors, they will tell you that using props needs very, very careful rehearsal. There is nothing worse than getting it wrong with a prop. As with the rest of your presentation, it is important to rehearse the use of props in front of someone.

CASE STUDY — NEVILLE CHAMBERLAIN

An Early Use of Props?

Many people have, no doubt, seen the black-and-white footage of British Prime Minister Neville Chamberlain returning from Munich in 1939, having had meetings with the German Führer Adolf Hitler. Chamberlain arrived at Heston Airport (the forerunner to Heathrow) at around 11.00 a.m. At that time the country was tense and agog to hear the news which Chamberlain was to proclaim as "Peace in our Time".

Historians will remember that Chamberlain was keen to reach an accommodation with Hitler. To communicate the impact of his agreement, Chamberlain pressed the newsreel camera teams into service, as it was the newsreels along with radio which provided the most instant medium for disseminating information.

Of course, at 11.00 a.m. at a little-used airport, there were very few people available to surround the Prime Minister as he made his momentous statement, so a "rent-a-crowd" consisting of local workers was brought in. Flanked by this crowd and officials, Chamberlain announced that he had an agreement with Hitler and held aloft a piece of paper announcing, "and this is the paper on which it is written".

Because the cameras needed to take close-up shots, this was done several times. The crowd clearly was unsure of what was expected of them, but Chamberlain's aides were in no doubt. As he held aloft the piece of paper yet again to stunned silence, one of them was heard to shout "Come on!" and with that the audience gave a cheer. This is probably the earliest recorded example of spin-doctors in action!

The laughable point is that it is said that the piece of paper held aloft was in fact Mrs Chamberlain's laundry list. Whatever it was, it was certainly effective for the time being, although as we now know the substance of the piece of paper turned out to be worthless. It might as well have been a laundry list.

Key Lesson*: Props can boost the impact of your message although, of course, if your message is wrong, it may come back to haunt you!*

Scan Converters and Data Projectors

When PowerPoint and similar computer graphics programs were first invented, the principal way of viewing the output of such programs was either directly on a computer screen, by hard copy print-outs, or print-outs on overhead view-foil acetates. Today, there are other alternatives available, the main ones being scan converters and data projectors. A scan converter is an electronic box which takes the output from a computer and re-configures it in such a way that it can be shown on an ordinary television monitor. This can be most useful when travelling with a presentation on, say, a laptop computer. Scan converters, which are relatively small in size, can then be used to hook your presentation output into a client's television monitor.

However, there are a number of drawbacks with scan converters. The first is that the resolution of an ordinary television monitor is much lower than that of a computer screen. One of the key elements in terms of resolution is the number of lines that make up the screen picture. Modern televisions, which are designed to receive broadcast signals, are configured to produce their images using 625 lines in the UK and continental Europe, 525 lines in North America. Computer screens have much finer resolutions, with their images being made up of well over 1,000 lines. This results in a television picture that is half as sharp as it would appear on a computer screen. Additionally, the conversion process itself can result in further degradation of the image. This degradation can be in terms of further loss of sharpness of image but also in colour distortion. Quite frequently, colours that appear bright and vibrant and in good contrast on a computer monitor can look dull, boring and hard to see when translated through a scan converter onto a television monitor. There is no way of predicting how scan converters will treat images from any given computer or laptop so they have to be used on a trial-and-error basis.

For this reason, it is important firstly to ensure that the images you choose to project are as clear and as large as possible. This particularly applies to text. Also, where colour and contrast are critical — in pie charts, for example — it is vital to check how the colours will actually appear on the equipment you have to use. One UK organisation with presentations to make in Northern Ireland once famously arrived at their first venue to discover that their carefully selected colour scheme had been transmuted to orange — a colour best avoided, particularly as they were presenting to a principally Catholic organisation.

A further complication when using scan converters is that many computers, particularly modern laptops, find it difficult to process their image through the converter. This can result in the image either not appearing at all or appearing totally distorted and unreadable. Another common glitch results in being able to project an image onto the television monitor but not on the laptop screen at the same time. Whilst this is not disastrous, it can make for a very difficult presentation and it rather defeats the object of a laptop screen in front of you if you have to keep looking at the scan-converted image on the TV monitor!

For these reasons, presenters are increasingly choosing to display their computer-generated images using *data projectors*. The earliest data projectors were made by companies such as Barco. These early machines were cumbersome and often sensitive, requiring a great deal of technical support. Often weighing 100lb and more, their mobility was strictly limited to being mounted on a trolley-like arrangement. They relied on a three-gun technique, whereby the images from three individual colour sources were projected onto a luminescent screen. Invariably, when they were moved they would go out of registration, resulting in a fuzzy image and requiring realignment of the guns to bring the picture back into focus — a time-consuming exercise. As a result, these machines tended not be moved at all and were hardwired into formal conference environments.

In the last ten years, data projectors have become smaller and smaller and the most modern ones now weigh as little as a few kilograms, with dimensions smaller than that of the average briefcase. It has now become a practical proposition to travel with a data projector, certainly by car if not by public transport.

The modern data projector offers you a number of advantages. The latest models work to software standards that ensure that in the main you can "plug and play". This allows any laptop to be plugged in and the machinery will sort out the images to be projected. However, data projectors can be sensitive to being switched on and off rapidly and they still need to be handled with care.

That said, data projectors are clearly the future when it comes to portable projection systems. However, they can be expensive, even though prices have been dropping. Whereas a scan converter can cost a few hundred pounds, a good data projector can set you back several thousand pounds.

Advantages and Disadvantages of Visual Aid Media

Visual Aid	Advantages	Disadvantages
35mm slides	• High quality image • Very effective when used correctly	• Inflexible; cannot change at last minute • Require very careful handling • Possibility of technical faults at venue
OHP slides	• Very effective when used correctly • Allow possibility of writing on slides, overlapping, or "reveals"	• Can be awkward to handle when there are a large number of foils • Can be time-consuming to set up • Possibility of technical faults at venue • Can look unprofessional if prepared or handled incorrectly

Visual Aid	Advantages	Disadvantages
Computer generation	• Flexible; can be easily adjusted at last minute • Add professional feel to presentation • Allows "build" effect and other transitional modes	• May require technical assistance • Compatibility problems can occur with earlier versions • Some possibility of technical faults at venue
Scan converters	• Easy to transport	• Compatibility problems can result in degraded image
Data projectors	• More standardised than scan converters	• Sensitive; require careful handling • Expensive
Props	• Effect can be devastating when used correctly	• Require much rehearsal • Can be distracting if used badly

Slide Packs

Traditionally, many presentations, particularly internal ones, are given with so-called *slide packs*. Here, the planned presentation slides are printed out in advance and handed to the audience who can then follow the presentation using the hardcopy print out of the slides. This, in principle, is fine, but in practice such presentations can go sadly wrong. This is particularly the case for internal presentations to superiors. What often happens is the presenter has prepared meticulously, only to find that within a few seconds of starting the presentation, the chief executive has flicked to the seventh or eighth slide and asked for an immediate explanation of what it means. This can totally throw the presentation and in some cases prevent the presentation being made properly at all.

Our advice is very strongly not to hand out slide packs in advance of your presentation. This way you give your audience absolutely no opportunity to become distracted through flicking through a slide pack. Wait until you have completed you presentation and hand out the slide packs as an *aide memoire* either straight after the presentation or as your audience leaves.

Key Points to Remember

- Preparation is vital.

- Make notes and boil them down to bullet points to be used on cards.

- Use the Rule of Five for your cards, using one card for each minute of speech.

- Visual aids are meant to enhance your presentation, not prop it up.

- Choose your visual aid medium according to the nature and importance of the presentation.

- Ensure that you are comfortable with the technology and that it will work on the day.

- Always have a hard copy standby.

- Rehearsal is key to success.

- Rehearse the use of props carefully.

- Do not hand out slide packs before your presentation.

Chapter 4

THE IMPACT FACTOR

I discussed earlier how 60 per cent of the effectiveness of a spoken presentation is actually nothing to do with the words themselves. Style, image, body language, tone of voice, choice of language, speed of delivery and a whole host of other factors serve to make up the majority of the impact of face-to-face spoken communications. It is therefore critical to maximise these factors if you are to have any hope of achieving the desired outcome of your spoken communication — namely to effect change in your audience.

Style

Your presentation starts the moment you get out of bed on the morning of your planned performance. In real terms, it actually starts the night before. Many business speakers ignore the fact that making a presentation is physically and mentally demanding. This is the case even if you have gone through the necessary steps of preparation. If you have failed to prepare, an attempt at any kind of decent performance is nothing short of gruelling. What chance have you therefore of making a stunning presentation if you have had a late night on top of too much to drink? Great performers, whether they be actors, opera singers or football players, know that physical and mental preparation is vital if they are to be at their peak for the event at which they are seeking to excel. Get an early night; avoid alcohol altogether, if you can, to ensure that you awake refreshed and ready for the rigours of the day.

There is an old cliché that says you never get a second chance to make a first impression, and also that most people have made their minds up about you in the first 30 seconds of your presentation. Both of these are true to a certain extent, so it is useful to put a little thought into planning how you are going to appear. In essence, image is a promise of delivery. In other words, your audience will have expectations raised about what they can expect just by looking at you. Studies have shown that the first aspect that will hit your audience will be your race or skin colour, swiftly followed by what sex you are and then your age. Clearly these factors are beyond our control, but we can do something about the next four factors. These are facial expression, body language, appearance and eye contact. Let us deal first with the factor which needs the most advance preparation and which is easiest to improve — appearance.

Here you must go through an exercise of self-analysis. Firstly, how do you want to be perceived? Secondly, how do you think the audience will perceive you?

Below is a range of characteristics. Choose two that you feel are most important to you personally and are therefore likely to best represent the way in which you want to be perceived by the audience:

• Educated	• Conservative	• Confident
• Successful	• Professional	• Consistent
• Youthful	• Mature	• Approachable
• Authoritative	• Creative	• Dynamic
• Quality	• Credible	• Experienced

You may intrinsically tend towards one or more personality types. However, for professional reasons, you may prefer to be seen as something else.

There is nothing dishonest about this, as very few of us are clear-cut in our individual personae. We all wear different masks depending on the company we are with. In normal social situations, we tend to don the appropriate mask automatically. For example, as mentioned in Chapter 2, men who in ordinary conversation with other men might use rather salty language automatically clean up their act when they find themselves in the company of women. For the majority of people, this process takes place without thought. There are those, however, who can forget themselves, often under the influence of alcohol. This loss of natural inhibition can occur in some for no reason at all and it is often brought about when an individual is under stress; the old problem of putting one's foot in it at just the wrong time in front of just the wrong person. Sufferers of a condition known as Tourette's syndrome have no such inhibitions at all and find themselves involuntarily using offensive language and speaking inappropriately with embarrassing and sometimes disastrous results. To a lesser extent, this happens to some individuals when making presentations. They sometimes struggle to find the appropriate mask and so need to prepare carefully. The key is to wear a mask which is effective in terms of the audience but that you also feel comfortable with. Good presenters learn how to feel comfortable in a number of masks and they achieve this through careful audience analysis and practice.

Look again at the table of personality characteristics above. Consider what an audience might be expecting in a business context. How does this compare to your honest analysis of your own perception of how you come across? Is there any disparity between the two? Repeat the exercise for a range of audiences. For example, the expectations of a Finance Direc-

tor and his or her team may indicate a different set of prefer-
ences to those of, say, a Marketing Director. Pragmatic presenters know they may have to adjust their approach to cope
with the expectations of the particular audience they are
seeking to sway.

What you wear is a key element in meeting audience expectations. You must dress the part. Over the years, our organisation has done a number of surveys on attitudes to
"dress-down Friday" exercises. This casual approach to the
last day of the working week was imported from the United
States about 15 years ago, principally with the new generation
of sunrise companies. Whilst in certain of the newer sectors,
information technology for example, it has been generally wel-
comed, a number of the more traditional areas of business
and commerce still find the concept very difficult. In particular, our surveys in the UK discovered that women are more
opposed to dress-down Fridays than men are. When we delved
further into this, it was found that the women were scathing
about the way in which their male colleagues approached
dress-down Fridays. They felt that most men did not know
how to dress down. Many had no real idea and felt that casual
was synonymous with having no style. Often individuals
ended up looking a shambles. At least, argued their female
counterparts, if the men wore conventional office attire such
as suits and ties, they could conform to some kind of uni-
formity and there was less scope for looking ridiculous.

For younger people, making compromises about dress can
come hard. But look at it from the point of view of the audience. Let us take an extreme case. Imagine that you are a patient lying in hospital awaiting the arrival of a surgeon whose
skill offers you the only hope of a return to full health. It is
Sunday and he is a keen gardener. How would you feel if he
arrived in a baggy sweater and his muddy gardening trousers,
with his nails caked in soil? Obviously, if you were desperate,

it probably would not matter at all how your surgeon looked. But clever medical practitioners know that giving confidence to the patient is a major part of helping them battle back to health. A good surgeon will have cleaned himself up and probably put on a suit and tie in order to build that necessary confidence in the mind of the patient.

There was a time when strict rules on business dress were laid down rigidly by some companies. In the 1960s and 1970s, you could always tell the man from IBM by his regulation white shirt and dark blue suit. Today, most companies are far more relaxed, but the wise presenter knows not to push this new-found freedom too far. Young people in particular should remember that many older people are inherently conservative. It is true that such prejudice can inevitably be regarded as an unfair infringement on the rights of the individual presenter. However, before you become too resentful, ask yourself the question, "Do I want to be right and stand on my dignity or do I want to be effective?" In the final analysis, in a business context at least, being effective is the watchword.

With the way things are at the moment in the general run of business, it is unlikely if you are a man that you will be making a presentation without a suit and tie. For women too, there are conventions about what you should wear, although these have always been less rigid. However, as we have discussed earlier, some companies are contributing to a change in accepted conventions, claiming that dressing casually helps managers concentrate on the brainpower and substance of an individual rather than their style. For most companies, the jury is either still out on this issue or they remain comfortable with convention.

All this makes it more confusing for the presenter who does not want to put a foot wrong. As with other aspects of presentation, planning and preparation are vital. Ask yourself the question, "What would make this audience feel most comfortable in terms of what I look like and how I dress?"

Whether you are male or female, any presentation you make will inevitably be a little special, so you may want to consider increasing your visual impact for the presentation. For men, this can be most easily achieved by wearing a tie brighter than you might normally wear in business. There is a danger, particularly for the more conventional businesses and the professions, that sober suits and ties can come across in a presentation as bland and boring. This is especially true for older men. Their greying hair often tops off an already grey image and a presentation environment only serves to accentuate that greyness. You must beware of appearing grey from top to toe; once you have acquired a reputation for greyness, it is very hard to shake it off, as former British Prime Minister John Major found to his cost.

It all started with his portrayal in the satirical television programme *Spitting Image* where the puppet representing Major was constructed entirely from grey latex. Despite the warmth and charm he exuded to all who met him in the flesh, it was the caricature which stuck and was fully exploited by opposition politicians who gleefully picked up and exaggerated the dowdy image, and he never managed to shake it off.

For women, the issue of image is slightly complicated. For them, a key factor is the *Triangle of Influence.* This affects men too, but it is most critical with women.

The Triangle of Influence

The Triangle of Influence is drawn with its point at the centre of your breastbone to form a triangle which takes in your eyes and all of your head, with its base running along the top of your head. It is critical because most of the audience's eyes will be drawn to this particular area. It is important, therefore, that you enhance your Triangle of Influence as much as practically possible. One traditional technique is to add a coloured scarf or a brooch to provide a lift to that area. However some forms of modern dress for women are more casual in approach and do not readily lend themselves to this technique so the clothes themselves must be chosen to flatter the Triangle of Influence.

The question of makeup is an increasingly thorny subject for many modern businesswomen. Women who do not normally wear makeup, or if they do very little, should recognise the need to add a little more makeup for presentational purposes, simply because it will add to their "brightness" factor. Many of today's businesswomen struggle with this, particularly if they hold beliefs that makeup potentially places them in a subservient role to men. However, makeup is often the only way of lifting the image to the levels required for a presentation and it is essential when appearing at large presentations on a stage where there are lights. The effect of lights will be to wash out any natural colour that you have and so you will have to use makeup if you are not to come across to your audience with a ghostly appearance. Unless you have tremendous natural colouring and a striking bone structure, you are going to have to face the fact that the application of makeup will be a key determinant of the success of your presentation.

It goes without saying that extra care should be taken to ensure that your clothes and shoes in themselves do not offer distractions to the audience. No matter how powerful the presentation, the audience will always be distracted by scuffed shoes, untidy hair, a showing slip or an annoying piece of thread dangling from a suit button, which all the audience is just dying to cut off. Other distractions come when you are sitting on stage with legs crossed. Many people find looking at the gap of pale skin between the top of a man's socks and his trouser leg unedifying (invest in longer socks, if only for presentations). Similarly, women have to guard against laddered tights (carry a spare pair).

Reasons Not to Buy

Above all we should be mindful that we can quite often turn people off by slipping up in any one of a number of areas. Here are some key turnoffs for men:

- Dandruff on clothes
- Dirty Hair
- Dirt on collars
- Missing buttons
- Badly kept hands
- Unflattering hairstyle
- Casual shoes
- Garish ties
- Suits unpressed, old
- Lack of personal hygiene (bad breath or body odour)
- Clothes which are inappropriate
- Unpolished and worn shoes
- Smoking odour/nicotine stains
- Aftershave which is too strong
- Patterned/brightly coloured socks
- Too many patterns mixed in shirt, tie and suit

For women, there are similar areas for turn off:

- Dandruff on clothes
- Dirty hair
- Dirt on collars
- Missing buttons
- Badly kept hands
- Laddered stockings
- Unflattering hairstyle
- Lack of personal hygiene (bad breath or body odour)
- Clothes which are inappropriate
- Unpolished and worn shoes
- Clothes too tight/short
- Smoking odour/nicotine stains
- Perfume which is too strong

By paying attention to these appearance details, you will portray a confident business image. When you make a presentation, small everyday faults in grooming can be magnified many times and will be noticed by many more people. People who regularly find themselves in the public eye, particularly those in the more glamorous areas such as television, will tell you that a large proportion of their mail is from people who comment on what they wear and how they look. Grooming is important. A good motto is:

Never neglect or you will lose respect

Remember, a mistake in your appearance can lead to a negative impression. To obtain the right style, whether you are male or female, all of the following must be examined and enhanced positively:

- Skin
- Hair
- Hands
- Teeth
- Figure
- Jewellery
- Spectacles
- Accessories

As we have discussed above, it is important not to give your audience cause to criticise your appearance, if only for the reason that while they are doing that they cannot be listening to what you are saying. However, another effect of dressing up is to make you feel special. This will help you add that extra something to your performance and really make it sparkle.

Dress in something that you feel makes you look good. This will add to your confidence when you come to do the presentation proper. I would recommend going through your wardrobe when you are not under pressure and sorting out the clothes and more importantly the combinations of clothes that work best for you. Many people have an innate sense of what looks right in a given situation, but if you are at all unsure, seek help and advice, preferably impartial. The key thing here is to plan what you are going to wear well in advance. Do not leave it to chance on the day or you may find that your favourite tie has a stain on it or that the outfit that particularly makes you feel good is away at the cleaners. Now that you have created the right image, you are ready to travel to your audience.

The Arrival

Plan well in advance your journey to the venue. Give yourself plenty of time, aiming to arrive at least an hour before your performance, longer if you are unfamiliar with the venue. There is nothing so off-putting to a speaker than to be delayed in traffic and arrive at the rush with just minutes to spare. You should allow enough time to familiarise yourself with the layout of the venue, how the slides change or computer controls work, adjust to the lighting, etc. At a large conference venue find out who is in charge of the technology and make a friend of him or her. They are your link to the audience and can mean the difference between success and failure. Remember, they have probably seen it all before. They will know how apprehensive you might be. Seek their advice and assistance. They can smooth your path and help counter many of the last minute difficulties you might have.

If you are a speaker at a large conference or seminar, try to find yourself a quiet area away from the crowds for the final half-hour before your planned performance. If it is a residential conference, then take the opportunity to lie down in your room for a few minutes. However, if there is a chance you will fall asleep, make sure you tell someone where you are or book yourself an alarm call ten minutes before you are due on stage. Letting someone know where you are is critical. Large performances at set-piece events such as seminars and conferences are very much team events. You may be the star turn, but avoid the temptation to play the prima donna. Ensure that you are co-operative and helpful. This includes not giving the organisers a heart attack because with just five minutes to go before you are due on stage, no one can find you and no one knows where you are!

The Stress of it all

No matter how polished you become in presentations, there is always an element of "butterflies in the stomach" as you approach the appointed hour. Many people ask how to get rid of the butterflies. The trick is not to try but instead to get the butterflies flying in formation. Stress comes in many forms, but the three principal ones are a feeling of overwhelming panic in your brain; shortness of breath and irregular breathing, which of course leads to a poor performance; and the shakes — physical lack of control on the muscles.

You can avoid over-stressing yourself by steering clear of coffee and other stimulants for at least two hours before the presentation is due. If you arrive on stage "wired" from excessive caffeine intake, you will find it harder to be in total control. It should go without saying that alcohol is unhelpful because although you may feel you are making a stunning performance, your audience may take a different view based on what they actually see!

Everyone suffers from the effects of nerves to a greater or lesser extent. The question is, how do you minimise the impact? There are techniques which, if practised regularly, can help greatly reduce the amount of stress you are under.

The first issue revolves around removing the fear of the presentation through removing the fear of the unknown. You hopefully will have done this through proper preparation and rehearsal. The effect on reducing your stress levels through ensuring that you have prepared properly cannot be over-emphasised. A great deal of angst can be avoided through proper preparation. The other issues relating to nerves can be relatively simply sorted. Let us start with breathing.

Breathe — *You'll Feel Better* and *Live!*

It is vital that you get your breathing correct in advance of going onto the platform. Otherwise, you run the risk of becoming short of breath through nerves. Shallow breathing will result in you only having available to you what is known as "residual air" to utilise in producing voice and volume. In essence, you will be using as little as a third of the total potential capacity of your lungs. All the main elements of effective voice control rely on having reserves of air. If you have too little air to play with, it is like trying to run a highly tuned car on low-grade petrol. You simply will not achieve the full potential of the performance. The effect of breathing on residual air will be that your voice will not carry as far as you would like it to; worse still, you also run the risk of your voice becoming squeaky and high-pitched.

To get your breathing right, take a few minutes before the presentation to sit calmly. Close your eyes and take deep breaths using your diaphragm (that is, let your stomach expand as you breathe in), in through the nose for three seconds, hold the breath for three seconds, and out through the mouth for three seconds. Repeat this several times, until your breathing starts once more to become calm, deep and more regular. A cycle of five or six times is useful. The effect of this process is to allow more oxygen into your bloodstream, which will in turn enliven your brain and promote a sense of well-being.

Don't Twitch!

Now we need to control your muscles. Here we use a technique much favoured by actors, singers and musicians. Imagine, if you will, a solo violinist who has to start his performance but who has the shakes. He will not sound too good. To relax your muscles and loosen up the tension, you need to close your eyes and concentrate on your ankles. In your mind's eye, allow them to go floppy. Then move your focus further up onto your knees; allow them to relax too. Continue moving this focus onto your thighs, and keep moving up your body, then up your spine until you reach the top of your spine. Consciously move your head forwards (not downwards) one or two centimetres. This has the effect of opening up the muscles around the voice box, which will enable you to develop your words more effectively and counteract the tendency for the throat to tighten and strangulate your words.

Finally, we need to calm your brain. Here we will employ some techniques drawn from the world of meditation. Simply sit quietly with your eyes closed and your fingertips together. Contemplate in your mind's eye the infinitesimally small gap between your fingertips. Think of nothing else; shut all other things out. This will have the effect of calming your brain and promoting a sense of well-being after just two or three minutes.

CASE STUDY — LESLEY GARRETT

Don't worry about your accent. Concentrate on your enunciation so you can be properly understood.

Can we in business pick up any tips on presentation from an opera singer? Of course. Especially when that singer is Lesley Garrett. Billed as Britain's favourite soprano, she has been wowing audiences throughout Britain and further afield for years with her highly palatable mix of romantic songs drawn from Rogers and Hammerstein and Lerner and Loewe, right through to Puccini and Carmen. I attended one of her concerts some time ago. Gliding on stage for all the world like a swan in a suitably diaphanous gown, she launched into a heart-stopping rendition of With a Song in my Heart *wonderfully backed by the Brandenberg Symphony Orchestra. Ten thousand people at Mottisfont in deepest, darkest Hampshire were mesmerised on a perfect late summer evening. And then she spoke.*

It was apparent immediately she was not from the South. Her beautiful bird-like singing voice was replaced by the unmistakably flat vowels of a solid South Yorkshire accent. Not for nothing is she known as the Diva from Doncaster. So many business presenters worry about their regional accents, fearing that they detract from their authority and belie a poor education. Lesley Garrett was unashamed of her roots and it did not matter a bit. Why? Because her diction was perfect. We could understand every word. And herein lies the lesson for all would-be public speakers. Whether you are speaking to ten people or ten thousand, enunciation is the key. As a trained singer, Ms Garrett knows how to form her words. We always find that people who have sung in school or church choirs speak more accurately as a result. It is all about opening your mouth.

She was good too in choosing her remarks. Offering up such a wide spread of vocal material runs a great risk of alienating the elite opera cognoscenti. But by being so engaging, she had us all, low and high brow alike, eating out of her hand by confronting the issue uppermost in our minds as the concert got off to a late start; the two-hour-plus traffic jams most people had sat in due to poor parking management by the organisers. You knew she had scored when she got all the audience of 10,000 people to sing Happy Birthday *to her father Derek, who was no doubt crimson with pride on that glorious evening. Now that's a class act!*

Key Lesson: *Don't worry about your accent. Enunciate clearly and after a few minutes, nobody will even notice it.*

Grasp the Technology

So many people assume that the technology will all be sorted out for them at any formal presentation. Do not rely on it. Most technicians are highly conscientious and, as we said earlier, it pays to make friends with them, but in the final analysis the face on which the flying omelette is likely to land will be yours. If you want to ensure that you are not to be defeated by the technology, it is important that you understand and become involved in what goes on.

Firstly, microphones. There are two basic forms of microphone: personal and stand microphones. There are advantages and disadvantages to both. Stand microphones have the advantage of being larger and more substantial. They are also normally hardwired to the amplification system, so there is less possibility of them going wrong. However, it does mean that you must stand where the microphone can adequately pick you up, which means there will be little scope for moving around the platform. You should check the location and adjustment of fixed microphones before the presentation. Once you are satisfied with the positioning, do not start fiddling with the microphone as soon as you mount the stage for real; it is annoying to the audience and looks unprofessional.

Personal microphones can be either hardwired or, as is more common these days, attached to a radio transmitter which you wear on your belt or in your pocket. Clearly, if they are hardwired you are still somewhat restricted in your movement, so wherever there is a risk that you will have to walk about, try to secure a radio microphone. Radio microphones make it possible to walk anywhere you like within range of the radio receiver. There are disadvantages, though. Many radio microphones still use frequencies that can often be shared with the local taxi firm. It is most off-putting when you are trying to make a stunning presentation to be interrupted by a "Roger, Roger," and confirmation of the pick-up at Number 23 Acacia Avenue!

Radio microphones need to be adjusted for voice level and bass cut. Also, they rely on battery power and batteries have an annoying habit of fading just at the wrong moment. To avoid this it is a good idea to exchange the batteries for new ones just before your presentation. The receiving unit which links into the sound system of the hall invariably has battery power too. Watch out also that your clothes don't block the microphone, muffling or distorting the sound. For these reasons, it is best to have a sound technician on hand whenever radio microphones are used.

Do not forget too that radio microphones can be embarrassing. When I worked in television, the sound technicians compiled over a number of years a library of recordings of inadvertent comments and trips to the lavatory made by studio guests. These poor unfortunates had wandered out of the studio oblivious to the fact that their activities were still being picked up and recorded courtesy of their still live radio microphone. Sometimes at a seminar you may have to speak a number of times and so will find yourself wearing your microphone semi-permanently. Radio microphones are simply disconnected by unplugging the microphone lead from the transmitter unit. Try to get into the habit of doing this when you leave the platform, but do not forget to connect up again before you go on, or you will have the sound technician tearing his hair out as he tries to fade up an unconnected microphone!

Radio microphones can present special problems for women. Whilst men can hide the transmitter unit inside a pocket, women's clothing often lacks such obvious places of concealment. Some sound technicians keep as part of their kit special belts and pouches to attach radio microphones to female presenters. These are normally worn under outer garments, so women need to remember that if they are to use a radio microphone, they need to dress appropriately so that such pouches do not stand out. A slinky evening dress may well be great for the occasion, but such attire can often look ridiculous if the carefully cut lines are interrupted by the bulge of a poorly concealed radio microphone.

It is a good idea to treat all microphones, radio or hardwired, as live and capable of transmitting anything you say to the widest possible audience. Former British Prime Minister John Major found this out to his embarrassment when, during a period of intense difficulty for him as he battled to keep various factions in his party rallied behind his government, he gave an interview to Independent Television News. He had concluded the interview with ITN's Michael Brunson and passed a comment to Brunson about how it was better to have what he described as the "bastards inside the tent pissing out rather than outside the tent pissing in" — referring to his reluctance to punish disloyal party members. At that stage, the television crew were packing up their equipment, so no doubt Mr Major felt his remarks were simple small talk and would go no further. Unfortunately for him, the microphones were still connected and a tape recorder was still running in the mobile control room parked outside Downing Street. His graphic description of Tory mischief-makers hit all the headlines the next day and informed political comment for months to come until the eventual defeat of the Conservative government.

One final point. Microphones are sensitive and of course vital to your effective presentation in that they are your final link with the audience. Resist the temptation to tap them to see if they are working. If you have a sound engineer, he will be listening on headphones. He will not thank you for tapping the microphone, as you will probably deafen him. Also, it is possible to break the microphone through tapping. Blowing on the microphone is equally distressing. If you really must test the microphone, simply place your hands over it and lightly touch it. That will be enough for you to realise whether it is working or not. Also, resist the temptation so beloved of northern working men's club comperes of mumbling "one, one two, one" into the microphone. It looks and sounds thoroughly unprofessional.

Sometimes a stand microphone will be positioned for you in order to pick your voice up for optimum effect. Accept this positioning, even if it may be a little awkward for you. A good sound engineer will adjust it to suit your height, the acoustic conditions of the room and of course the power and style of your voice. He will also be adjusting it to avoid feedback or "howl round", which are the terms given to the terrible whine you sometimes get when the sound of the speaker feeds back into the microphone and round continuously. Where this is a problem, you may find yourself having to speak much more closely into the microphone than you would normally feel comfortable with. This can be a particular problem if you have what are known as powerful *plosives*. These are words which have strong beginnings formed by the lips starting with letters such as P and B. Powerful plosives can quite literally explode onto the microphone, resulting in a pop. You can counter this by moving the microphone further away or learning to turn slightly away from the microphone for plosive words. Again, accept the advice of the sound engineer, whose job it is to ensure that you get the very best out of the sound system.

Once the microphone is set up for you, do not mess about with it. I once witnessed a captain of industry who on mounting the platform to speak simply pushed the carefully positioned microphone to one side. He then proceeded to deliver his presentation totally off-mike for the next 25 minutes!

Getting on Stage

Your performance proper starts the moment you get up from your seat and walk to the point at which you are to make your presentation. If you are making a semiformal presentation, then your performance starts the moment you enter the room. When it is your turn to speak, do not be in too much of a hurry. Many great orators of the past, from Marx to Mussolini, would stand and look at their audience for several seconds before actually opening their mouths. In a business environment, one or two seconds to establish your presence is all that is required, but it is important that you do take that time to establish presence.

We talked earlier about how facial expressions are a key element of the first impression your audience forms of you. Unless the circumstances genuinely dictate otherwise (you are giving a funeral oration or announcing a set of redundancies), you should always aim to smile, even before you open your mouth to utter the first word of the presentation. Smiling, as we know, is one of the best ways of engaging your audience. It puts them at ease and demonstrates a friendly approach, so smile, "even though your heart is breaking", as the old song goes. Of course, this advice is easy to give and hard to put into practice, especially during those first nerve-wracking moments when your heart is trying to leap out of its rib cage! However, you must school yourself to start your presentations with a smile. One obvious technique is to draw a "smiley" at the top of your notes to remind you.

It is important that you anchor yourself physically at the start of your presentation. You should stand with your feet one and a half feet apart and for the first 30 seconds or so remember to stand still. There is always a tendency when people are nervous to swivel their hips or to rock about or step back and generally telegraph to the audience that you are not comfortable being there in front of them. Above all, stand still.

A word about lecterns. They are there to support your notes; they are not there to support you. It is important to adjust the height correctly. Ideally, the bottom lip of the lectern should be level with your navel. Start from this position and, if possible, ask someone to check how it looks ahead of the audience entering the room. If you are on a stage looking down on the audience, you will want to lower the lectern slightly. If you are in an auditorium where the audience is looking down on you, you can raise the lectern. Sometimes people with impaired eyesight raise the lectern to position their notes closer. Whilst you can allow a little latitude on this, it is better to have your notes written out in larger letters rather than obscure too much of your body with the lectern. Lectern adjustment is particularly critical if you are following another speaker. A few years ago during the American bicentennial celebrations, the Queen of England found herself following US President Clinton to the lectern. The lectern had been adjusted to the President's 6'2", so when the Queen, at only 5'3", stepped up to deliver her speech, the only thing the assembled company could see was her very fetching canary yellow hat!

Avoid the temptation to grip the lectern. Often they are not very sturdy and I have seen a lectern totally demolished by a nervous speaker. This will surely spoil your day. Stand behind or to one side of the lectern and do not lean on it or grip it.

What do you do with your hands? We have researched this and clearly there are a number of things you can do with your hands. Some of these hand positions appear defensive, some look slovenly and some hand positions can be perceived as arrogant. There is only one real thing to do with your hands at the beginning of a presentation so that you do not look awkward. You have to put your hands in what we call the *home position*. They should be placed one on top of another over your navel. This is a position from which you can then use your hands to speak and emphasise your spoken words.

If you are seated, round a table for example, then a different home position applies. It is important when sitting at a table to ensure that your hands are always on view. Indeed, in some cultures, particularly in the Middle East, hiding your hands can result in your audience mistrusting you. Apparently, this stems from the ancient fear that you might be concealing a weapon. Although this is less likely in modern times, old traditions die hard. Ensure that you keep your hands and arms on the table overlapping each other.

Venue

Some people, particularly in professional firms, like to make presentations to prospects on their own business premises rather than those of the prospects. This has advantages and disadvantages. The advantages are that you will know the equipment and will feel relaxed in the environment. The disadvantage is that you will become too relaxed and fail to treat the presentation as the performance it truly is. You need to guard against this if you are to be successful. Remember, it may be on your premises, but it is still the prospect who is potentially buying and they are to all intents and purposes new to the environment and to your presentation.

Be Positive

When you finally open your mouth, remember that you have very few words to play with in terms of the receiving time when compared to the written word. It is important therefore to stress the positive rather than the negative. Above all, this means using extremely positive language; active verbs rather than passive ones; "We will do this" rather than "This will be done". You must avoid the use of what we call "mandarin". You will have heard it. It is very similar to that used by Sir Humphrey in the award-winning BBC series *Yes Minister*.

> "We have taken due cognisance of all the issues that have to be factored into this ongoing equation and not-withstanding the previous views held by other interested parties we have to tell you that our own opinion is not necessarily unadjacent to that which we expressed in the ultimate month."

Of course, you would not dream of speaking like that; however, what you might do is use quite a lot of jargon. Remember my definition of jargon in Chapter 2 (a word or phrase which just one person in the audience does not understand)?

Look Them in the Eye!

Eye contact is vital during any successful presentation. The definition of eye contact is looking at someone in the audience for not less than two seconds and not more than five seconds. If it is less than two seconds, then you run the risk of coming across as shifty. More than five seconds of staring at an individual is calculated to make them feel most uncomfortable.

Eye contact is critical at three key points in your presentation: the beginning, when you are seeking to engage the audience; the end, when you want to leave them with a lingering message from you; and at any other point of passion within the presentation.

Let me stress again that eye contact is about looking at individuals in the audience, not trying to cover the whole audience. It is definitely not about "spraying your eyes around the audience like a machine gun". You can use eye contact to bring back into engagement an individual or group in the audience who you feel may be slipping away in terms of attention. Even if an individual has their head down and you look at the top of their head for a few seconds, it is amazing how quickly you can get that individual to look up at you and return your eye contact. Once you have done so, you will find that they will be once more engaged with your presentation. What is more, the act of bringing one person in a disaffected group back into contact can amazingly result in also bringing back other members of the group.

One thing to avoid is a piece of advice I heard given some years ago, which is simply to address your remarks to the clock at the back of the room. You will certainly fail to engage the audience, even if you do manage to finish on time!

Action

It is important to come across as animated; this is because humans are sentient beings. Their brains are stimulated by action. This why television is more popular than radio. We are more interested in and more stimulated by what we see rather than what we hear. So you must put action into your presentation. But you must get it right: the action must support what you are saying. Your body language must not give the impression that you are uncomfortable being in front of your audience. Often you see inexperienced presenters using actions which are the exact opposite to what they mean. For example, throwing their arms out wide when they are talking about "narrowing the options". Or they get out of kilter in terms of timing, using the correct action but failing to synchronise it with the words they are speaking by making the gesture either too early or too late. Another common fault is regular, rhythmic but inappropriate hand movements, which can range from a nervous twitch through to a series of random gestures unconnected with the thrust of the presentation. Such movements usually annoy the audience and detract from the effectiveness of your presentation. Such movements are often the hardest for the speaker to spot for himself. Here, consultation really pays off and it is a good idea to seek advice on whether you are falling into any of the traps outlined above.

CASE STUDY — ARTHUR SCARGILL

You need hands!

During the 1970s and 1980s in Britain, the leader of the National Union of Mine Workers, Arthur Scargill, led several strikes against the government's plans to scale down mining in the UK. He was then, and still is, an orator par excellence with a very loyal bedrock of support from miners, particularly in his native Yorkshire.

One of the key elements he employed to make his speeches more powerful was an effective use of hand movements. On one occasion, having marched in a rally through pouring rain, he stood up at the platform to implore his audience, which consisted of both miners and other workers, to remain solid for the cause of the National Union of Mine Workers. This is what he said:

> *"This time Britain's miners are not just fighting for jobs in the mining industry. Don't leave us isolated. Support us all the way until we reverse this policy."*
>
> *In the space of just fifteen seconds, Scargill used a whole range of hand movements thus:*
>
> *Firstly both hands are held up almost in a supplication to the audience. "This time" he says, "Britain's miners are not just fighting for jobs." Here he pushes his left hand to the side as if dismissing this issue. "Don't leave us isolated," he implores his audience with outstretched, upturned hands, drawing them towards him. Then comes the power punch with both hands and clenched fists. "Support us all the way." He then wags one finger away from the audience in a dictatorial manner and to rising cheers. "Until we reverse this Tory policy".*
>
> *You probably would choose not to use all those gestures in the space of fifteen seconds, but the movements are worth remembering and practising for when you do have an opportunity of employing one or more of them to add emphasis to your spoken words.*

Remember too that your language must pass the pub test; you would not go into a bar or public house and cry out,

> "Landlord, draw for me a pint of your finest foaming ale in order that I might partake of it and thus slake my thirst."

Such a use of language would get a fairly swift and short response from the publican and you would be less likely to be served with the drink you desire.

Instead, you should be using short simple words and constructions. Use the word "show" rather than "demonstrate"; instead of "enable" use "help"; in place of "prior to" try "before".

Timing

Timing is critical in a presentation. I have already discussed that you are more likely to be forgiven for under-running than for over-running. Another key element of timing is the power of the pause. The pause is one of the most influential devices used in effective spoken communications. A pause just before a word or phrase and just after can highlight the word or phrase. A pause can be used to change gear or direction in a presentation. When answering questions, a pause can be used to give credibility and credence to the question and also to the value of the answer that you are about to give. In short, use pauses throughout your presentation to add weight to what it is you are trying to say.

CASE STUDY — MARTIN LUTHER KING

Beyond your wildest dreams?

Passion, timing and personal involvement wins the day. Everyone remembers the "I have a dream" speech which Martin Luther King made on the steps of the Lincoln Memorial in Washington DC, just a few months before he was assassinated. Even today, three decades later, it still makes the hairs stand up on the back of the necks of those who listen to the speech, so poignant and fiery is it. This is a speech aimed at promoting the civil rights movement and calling for an end to racial discrimination. Its most telling lines come about 17 minutes into the speech:

"I have a dream that my four little children will one day live in a country where they are not judged by the colour of their skin but by the content of their character. I have a dream today."

In themselves, the words are powerful enough, because Dr King is advancing his message through a very personal experience involving his "four little children". Such imagery is guaranteed to move even the hardest of hearts.

Coupled with his tremendous use of timing, it really is a tour de force. In those 39 words, Martin Luther King pauses for in excess of six full seconds. This is how he actually delivered the speech:

"I have a dream [PAUSE, FOUR SECONDS] that my four little children [PAUSE, TWO SECONDS] will one day live in a country where they will not be judged by the colour of their skin but by the content of their character. I have a dream today."

Towards the end of the paragraph, Dr King employs three other oratorical techniques. From ". . . but by the content of their character" to the end of the paragraph he speeds up to stress the urgency of his demands. He also repeats his "I have a dream" motif for added emphasis. Finally, his voice gradually rises in volume and force throughout the speech, ending on a crescendo.

There are very few pieces of oration to match such a powerful use of the pause.

Key Lesson*: Martin Luther King learned his speaking style in the churches of the Southern Baptist Bible belt of the Deep South. Clearly that is not a tradition shared by all, but we can all learn to use pausing more effectively, and no matter how long you think the pause really is when you are speaking, it will actually be much more effective if it is longer rather than shorter.*

Key Points to Remember

- Get a good night's sleep before the day of the presentation; avoid alcohol.

- Plan and prepare your appearance carefully; dress appropriately and ensure you are well groomed.

- Sit calmly for a few minutes before your presentation, concentrating on your breathing.

- Check microphones before the presentation.

- Maintain eye contact with your audience at key moments in the presentation.

- Be animated and lively, but don't go over the top.

- Use pauses and timing to add impact.

Chapter 5

ON YOUR FEET:
DELIVERING A STUNNING PRESENTATION

Up to now we have dealt with all the necessary steps needed to get you on your feet and working well. In terms of being effective with your spoken communication, you are about 80 per cent of the way there. However, anyone who has ever had to speak in public has horror stories about things that can go wrong during a spoken presentation. In this chapter, we will look at some of the more common difficulties and offer suggestions on how you can overcome them.

Getting Started

Many people say that no matter how well they prepare, they just cannot seem to get off to a good start. Those initial couple of minutes are just purgatory, when the speaker wishes the ground would open up and swallow him or her. Getting off to a flying start is tough for most people. However, starting on the right foot is essential if your presentation is to have a feel of quality to it. It is a real skill and one that all aspiring speakers must develop. Some call this skill "Breaking the ice"; others "Engaging the audience". I prefer to call it "Going from 0–60 mph in half a second", as this more precisely describes what is required.

Developing such a skill is particularly difficult for those who for most of their professional lives are expected to work in a steady, diligent, almost contemplative way. Take lawyers, for example. Their advice is expected to be impartial and arrived at after due deliberation. In other words, their clients expect their opinions to be considered. In the normal run of their commercial activity, they are not expected to rush at things. It is the same with engineers. If, for example, they are constructing a bridge, we expect them to take care and pay particular attention to detail. After all, the bridge has to be properly constructed and stand the test of time. We certainly do not want them to rush the structure up. With these and other professions, it is almost a case of deliberately slowing down the faster-moving functions of the brain to ensure that the contemplative side of the thought process wins out.

Unfortunately, public speaking requires that the brain functions much more swiftly and good speakers have to be quick at thinking on their feet, come what may. Of course, practice makes perfect, but unfortunately many speakers cannot afford the luxury of practising on clients and prospects. So what to do? One solution is to start young and actively seek out less high-profile occasions to try out your speaking ability. Debating clubs in schools and colleges are ideal starting points. Organisations such as the Junior Chamber of Commerce in the UK can give young would-be speakers the opportunity of flexing their vocal chords in a relatively non-threatening environment, or at least certainly one where the impact of failure is minimised. At one time, very few organisations offered such opportunities. Fortunately, there is now a discernible trend in this direction, with more and more similar organisations putting emphasis on facility with the spoken word. There is, however, still a long way to go and there are still a vast number of people who have had little or no experience of public speaking from a young age.

So, back to the present. Let us assume you have not had much experience in your youth and you lack that necessary confidence to deliver a speech or presentation without feeling that nerves are going to destroy the performance and you with it. Despite this, you have been requested to speak and there is no alternative but to go ahead and do your very best. You have prepared your presentation and the hour is upon you. You stand up to speak, open your mouth to launch into your delivery and then it all goes blank. Remember that there are two things which you are unlikely to forget, no matter how pressured you feel. Firstly, whether it is morning, afternoon or evening and, secondly, your name. So you should at least be able to get out the opening of your presentation:

"Good morning/afternoon, ladies and gentlemen.
My name is . . ."

Next hit them with the headline:

". . . and I'm here to talk to you today
about . . . which will . . ."

And here you tell them about the stunning benefits that what you have to say will deliver to them. Remember, in spoken communications you have to give them the cherry on the cake first. In other words, start off with,

"Hey! Guess what . . . ?"

All of the above sounds well and good, but if you are still concerned about drying up, then it is a good idea to learn the first minute or so of your presentation off by heart. This way, you will get off to a flying start and be able to go from zero to sixty miles an hour in half a second flat. Most people find that once they can get through that first minute, they are up and running. The rest of the presentation (given adequate preparation and rehearsal) will flow easily after that.

Remember to smile and if you are nervous, choose a friendly face in the audience if possible and smile at them.

Remember to use eye contact right at the very beginning to ensure you engage your audience. Make sure you do not bury your head in your notes; nothing telegraphs a sense of nervousness and uncertainty to an audience more effectively than a speaker with his head down, ploughing on regardless!

But I Am Still Shaking!

This happens and it happens to the best of speakers from time to time. Sometimes, for almost inexplicable reasons, even the most self-assured people get the shakes. It has happened to me on one or two occasions and, rather like earthquakes, it is devilishly difficult to predict with any precision exactly when it will happen. Different factors throw different people. When I was appearing every day on live television, I seldom felt nervous, despite the inner knowledge that I was being beamed out to millions of people. However, doing a recorded piece to camera on location could easily be upset by just a handful of interested onlookers. Perhaps it was something to do with seeing the whites of the eyes of the audience.

Some people are thrown by large audiences, some by small but "important" audiences. Some speakers find it difficult in a formal auditorium talking, in effect, to a black void with limited scope for actually seeing the audience. However, while some people find the glare of stage lighting off-putting, others positively welcome the fact that you cannot see the audience. One thing is certain; sooner or later you will find your speaking nemesis and it is sure to be one which turns your legs to jelly and gets your knees knocking.

So what to do? The first thing to remember is that it is important to anchor yourself. Although I have said previously that it is best not to grip the lectern, you can break that rule to temporarily steady yourself. Make sure, though, that the lectern is sturdy enough. Some are very flimsy and the last thing you want is to transfer your shakes to the lectern and demolish it because it is not strong enough. If your legs are shaking and your knees knocking, try to consciously lock them into position. Above all, try to keep still and not give in to the impulse to swivel about. Keep still until you have recovered your composure, then ensure that any moves you make are purposeful and add value to your presentation in terms of emphasis.

Your hands, of course, should be in the home position — gently folded just above your navel. Make sure they are flat and do not intertwine your fingers. Inevitably, if you do and you are nervous, you will start to wring your hands and your white knuckles will be a dead giveaway to your state of internal turmoil! Keep your hands in the home position and forget about them until you feel confident enough to use them to express yourself with more emphasis.

Remember to breathe. If you start taking short, shallow breaths, you will only add to your stress. Breathe deeply, through the nose if you can remember to. Proper breathing offers a real solution to many presentational problems. Apart from making you feel better, you will find that correct breathing forces you to pace your presentation and add proper pauses to the flow of information. It will also stop your voice narrowing and going up in pitch — a real risk for people under pressure, particularly for women. If you can get your breathing right, the rest will follow.

Trying to Do Too Much

It is amazing how many speakers make life difficult for themselves through being poorly organised. When it comes to using props and visual aids, the reason is often down to co-ordination between the parts of the brain that control speech and those that control movement. Many people struggle when asked to perform more than one task at a time, especially if one of the functions is unfamiliar to them. You may remember the rather unkind comment made of former United States President Gerald Ford when he was described as, "the kind of guy who finds it hard to walk and chew gum at the same time". We all suffer to a greater or lesser extent from the same affliction and for many adults this lack of co-ordination can manifest itself for the first time when speaking in public. It is all down to the extra workload put on a brain unused to such challenges. The good news is the brain has tremendous capacity to learn how to cope with such challenges.

You are asking a great deal of your brain when you get up to speak. First, you have to prepare to speak with the correct voice in terms of pitch and power. Then you have to take in information through your eyes from your notes. If you are using slides, you have to remember to move the slides on at the appropriate time. It is the same with computer-generated slides, and with OHPs, it can be even more challenging as you wrestle with the large acetates, trying to get them on and off the overhead projector in a smooth and dignified manner.

So many things can go wrong as you try to speak. A common problem with slides is keeping your finger on the forward button too long or, because of the shakes, inadvertently pressing the button twice and skipping a slide. Then you can get into a real tizzy trying to get the slides to go back. A tip here for PowerPoint users: always use the forward or right arrow on the keyboard rather than the left-hand mouse click to advance the slides. If you find you have inadvertently gone on too far, pressing the back or left arrow will take you smoothly back to the previous slide. If you are using a left hand mouse click to forward the slideshow, a right hand mouse click will only add to your panic as, instead of taking you back to the previous slide, it throws a dropdown menu onto the screen which will require even more mouse clicks through the offered options to put things right. You can do without all this when you are attempting to make a meaningful presentation.

If you are using props, it gets more complicated still. All actors stress the need to rehearse the use of props. You must rehearse too, but before you do that, you must organise your presentation space. We have discussed earlier how to place an OHP. The same principles apply to other presentational aids you might use. The key here is to avoid clutter.

Card Management and Organisation

The same principles apply when it comes to card management. Your eyes have the capacity to process a million bits of information a second. The problem is, the part of the brain which interprets the signals from the eyes finds it difficult to discriminate instantly between useful and useless information, so if they see clutter, they will try to process clutter and make sense of it. This will only serve to confuse your brain and risks more co-ordination problems. So, even if you have to rewrite your cards several times, make sure you have a clean and legible set of cards to present from, with no scribbling or crossings out. The golden rule is:

Organise clearly and simply

Of course, to follow this rule, you will need to take time. So many speakers rush up, spread out their materials willy-nilly and launch straight into their presentation. It is a recipe for disaster.

There are at least three or four ways of handling your cards during a presentation. In my experience, only one works really well, while some of the others can actually mar your performance. You will have all your notes in bullet point form on cards obeying the Rule of Five and, as we have already discussed, the cards will be pristine. The cards should be numbered, preferably in the top right hand corner. Arrange the cards in two piles on the lectern. Try always to be prompted off the card on the top of the left-hand pile, with the unused cards face up in order in a pile on the right. This means that, as we naturally read English from left to right and from top to bottom, you will first be prompted from the left-hand card. Once you have scanned down to the bottom of the left hand card, you then move across to the top of the right-hand card. Once you find yourself being prompted from the right-hand card, unhurriedly slide it across to the left-hand pile to reveal a new card on the right-hand pile. You are now being prompted once again from what has become the left-hand card. The sliding across of the cards from the right-hand pile should be done in your own time to avoid one of the curses of presentations — punctuation by card.

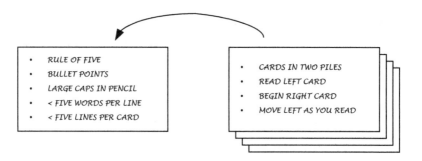

This sounds complicated on paper, but the process is straightforward. It results in a smooth handling of the cards and, with a little practice, can greatly reduce the stress associated with speaking from bullet point notes. The method outlined above is also less likely to cause distraction to the audience. You want them to be focusing on you. You do not want them worrying themselves about what is happening with your cards.

Many people punch a hole in the corner of each card and then hold them together with a treasury tag. Whilst this is a good method of ensuring you do not get your cards out of order, I recommend removing the tag before your presentation and using the two-pile method outlined above.

I am often asked about holding cards in the hands during the presentation, the argument being that this gives you something to do with your hands. This is true, but it also prevents you from using your hands effectively to express yourself more forcefully and emphasise key points. Much better to have the cards on the table or lectern in front of you. Some people complain that it is difficult to read the cards at a distance, particularly if you normally wear spectacles. The answer here is quite simply to write in larger block capitals.

Autocue

Sooner or later if you become a seasoned speaker, you will be offered the magic of Autocue. Autocue is one of the trade names given to that method of prompting which enables the speaker to continue to look at the audience because their notes or script are projected directly into their eye line to the audience.

Autocue is often seen as the salvation of nervous conference speakers. In fact, conferences and seminars are the most common scenarios where you might encounter Autocue — see Chapter 10. Many clients have come to us facing the prospect of a conference or seminar presentation and announced, "It is not so bad because at least I'll be able to use Autocue." Autocue, or its rival Portaprompt, are terrific aids to a speaker but only if used correctly and only if the speaker is capable in the first place of speaking *without* Autocue. Some clients come to us asking to be taught how to use Autocue when they have had no training and indeed demonstrate little competence in speaking without such prompting aids. Our response is invariably the same. First we will teach you to speak effectively, then we will teach you how to use Autocue. Use of Autocue in the wrong hands is rather like computerising a poor office system. All you do is speed up the disaster!

There are two key ways in which you can use Autocue. Firstly, you can have a full script with every word written out exactly as you would speak it. Again, use the methodology described in earlier chapters to arrive at such a script. Secondly, you can use Autocue simply to have your bullet points placed in a position where you do not find yourself looking down. Frankly, this second option provides very little advantage over having your bullet points on cards and our advice would be that, given the choice, you would be better off with cards than with Autocue. However, if you have a particularly complicated presentation with lots of slides and demonstrations, etc. and you want to be word perfect for political or regulatory reasons, you would be well advised to use a full script on Autocue.

The way both Autocue and Portaprompt work is to project your script onto a glass screen in your eye line, set in such a way as to make you appear to be looking directly at the audience. What the speaker actually sees on the screen is three or four lines, comprising no more than three or four words on each line, often fewer. The audience, of course, sees nothing except an unobtrusive thin glass plate which they readily get used to and ignore. In rare cases, a curved glass screen is erected around the speaker and the image of the words is projected several times so they can be viewed from whichever angle the speaker chooses to face the audience. This system has been used by US Presidents, and it is alleged that their glass has been bullet-proofed!

Looking at just three or four lines of text on Autocue screens can be most disconcerting to the newcomer to this form of presentation aid. An easy trap to fall into is to become fixated on the words themselves and so what the audience tends to see is a glassy stare flicking rapidly from left to right as the words are followed. The key element of any prompting system is the operator. Usually these individuals are highly experienced and very co-operative. Their job is to follow you and adjust the movement of the Autocue to your speaking speed. A good operator will ensure that the current line you are speaking is always in the same position on the screen. This is achieved by setting a moveable cursor, usually a third of the way down from the top of the screen (you can ask the operator to adjust the cursor to your own convenient setting, but a third down is the best position for most speakers).

What you will notice when working with an Autocue operator is that the words do not move at a consistent speed. The line will move and then stop and then move again. This is because we do not speak consistently and smoothly and a good operator will be taking great pains to ensure that he or she follows you as precisely as possible. Newcomers to Autocue often expect to have the words scroll at a consistent rate; an average speaking speed. This simply will not work. Just speak normally and let the operator do their job in following you.

On your part, it is important that you do not digress from the script, as the Autocue operator may struggle to follow you; after all he or she is a prompting operator, not a clairvoyant! In essence, you have to be very disciplined to use Autocue effectively and some speakers find this places them too much in a constricting straitjacket.

The words can be projected in two ways. Normally there are two, sometimes three, clear glass screens placed in your eye line just in front of the lectern. On the floor beneath these screens are television monitors which display the prompting output; this is in turn reflected onto the glass screens. (Incidentally, the TV monitors are configured electronically to display the script in mirror image text, which of course projects the "original" text onto the screens.) The screens must be adjusted to suit your eye line so that you appear to be looking towards the middle of the auditorium. Herein lies a difficulty vis-à-vis eye contact. We have mentioned in earlier chapters that eye contact needs to be made with various members of the audience at various times. One of the problems with an Autocue system is that invariably your eyes will be fixed at one given level in the audience, and the ability to look up and down the levels of the audience will be severely limited. This is a particular issue in a conference theatre where the seats are steeply raked. However, you will be able to look left and right and this will greatly help give the impression of casting around the audience and taking them all in. It will also help hide the natural propensity for the eyes to flick left and right, as head movements will disguise this. Such movements of the head are vital if the speaker is to look natural. If you fix on one screen for more than a few seconds, the audience will spot your eyes moving from left to right as you follow the text and the illusion will be shattered. They will know you are reading to them, not talking to them and persuading them from the heart.

When using transparent glass screens you are somewhat tied to the lectern position and there is little scope for major movement. However, another way for the Autocue images to be projected will be directly on television monitors (this time the electronics are adjusted so you get a true text image, not a mirror image) normally placed on the floor and towards the edge of the stage. This enables you to depart from the lectern and walk about the stage. It is also possible for these monitors to be placed elsewhere in the audience in such a way that you can see them but the audience cannot. They can also be placed on stands so the monitors are at a more convenient eye line. Naturally, the audience cannot see through the monitors so they have to be placed at greater distances than the glass screen so speakers need good eyesight to read the text or the text has to be adjusted so you see larger text but fewer lines.

A third way for Autocue to be projected will be onto a glass screen slung in front of a TV camera. This is the system used in television studios. At one time, cameras tended to have been used only in very large and important conferences but as the price of the technology continues to fall, they are increasingly used in many smaller seminars with the image of the speaker being projected on to a large screen. On these occasions, speakers often opt to ignore direct eye contact with the audience and rely on their screen image to create the necessary eye contact to get their message across. One is tempted to ask: "Why make the presentation at all; why not just make a video and reduce the angst of a live performance?" Indeed some senior executives are doing just that and often appear to be beaming in from on high via satellite or more usually on video. (By the way, if you do opt for the satellite route, ensure you have a video back-up for when the gremlins strike!)

All these arrangements will of course vary from venue to venue and will need to be thoroughly checked out. You will need at least one run-through on the Autocue with your operator to ensure that you are perfectly synchronised and there are no surprises for either of you. Remember, you rely on him or her to ensure that your presentation is properly delivered.

On the stage itself you will need, as I have mentioned, to ensure that you have the glass screens properly adjusted to your eye line. This can present problems if you are one of a number of speakers. Some prompting systems overcome this by having electrically adjusted remote controlled screens. These can be pre-set to specific speaker heights. Again, you need to find out in advance how this is going to happen and ensure that, come what may, either remotely or manually the screens are adjusted to suit your eye line. If the screens cannot be adjusted automatically, then ensure that a stage hand does the adjustment for you. Fiddling with the screens yourself will only detract from your on-stage authority. Remember, you cannot guarantee nerveless hands just before you launch into your speech. If one of the screens slips and breaks, it will thoroughly spoil your day!

When you finally make your presentation, remember to speak at your natural pace. The Autocue operator will follow you.

What if I Dry During the Presentation?

Even if you get off to a flying start, there are occasions when you suddenly find yourself at a loss for words. Sometimes it happens because you catch the eye of someone in the audience and this puts you off. Everyone dries at one stage or another in their speaking career. The trick is not to make a big thing of it. When you cannot think of the next thing to say, stop talking. It may seem obvious, but this means closing your mouth. So many people forget this and the audience is treated to a series of long drawn-out "Errs" and "Umms" or to what is known as "goldfishing", where the speaker opens and closes his mouth noiselessly just like a goldfish in a bowl. Do not be tempted to waffle and above all stay calm and do not panic. Just stop talking, look down at your notes and find out where you are. Once you have found your place, pick up a new prompt, look up at your audience and start again. Doing all this will take a little time but, although, it will seem like an eternity to you, the speaker (during which time you *will* want the ground to open up and swallow you!), it will in reality only be a matter of seconds. Most audiences will sympathise with your plight. Indeed, many will no doubt be thinking, "There but for the grace of God go I"!

Often, drying occurs when you have fallen into the trap of speaking ahead of your notes. This can be caused as much by over-rehearsal (and therefore over-confidence) as under-rehearsal. It particularly affects highly intelligent and quick-thinking presenters. The problem they face is that they continually want to update and amend their presentation with new ideas which hit them "on the hoof". In short, they suffer from having ideas in the head. All too often, because these ideas have not been thought through, let alone rehearsed, they result in you following an unknown route and can often totally destroy the planned impact of the presentation.

In the world of the theatre, there is a clear division between playwright and actor. The playwright is there to pen the words and the actor is required to learn the lines and speak them with dramatic effect. The actor is not expected to change them or add in new ideas of his own. In the world of business, it is important to recognise that the presenter is usually both playwright and actor. However, the roles have to be kept separate and there comes a point when you have to stop your playwriting activities and move into the acting role. At that point, you "put your presentation to bed", to borrow a phrase from the world of newspapers. After this point, you should only make changes which are absolutely vital and these will usually be changes of fact rather than style or emphasis. What you should not do is suddenly start a whole new train of thought. For one thing, you do not have the time to effectively work through your new ideas and secondly, as I have said before, "They'll never know what you never said".

Once you have moved into the role of actor, drop your pen and stick to the script. You should be using the rehearsal time to hone the style of what it is you want to say and ensuring that you say it with the right emphasis and passion.

If, despite all the above, you still dry, then take stock and look at your prompt cards. Do not attempt to continue until you have found out where you are. Gather your thoughts, take a deep breath and start again. As I said earlier, it will seem to you that you have taken an age to do all this but many of our clients have been amazed when looking back at a video of themselves to see how short the pause is in reality when viewed from the point of view of the audience. If you have left something out, it may not be necessary to go back over it. The presentation will probably survive the odd omission. Remember, the audience will be none the wiser as long as you do not point up your mistake.

If you get completely stuck, then you may feel the need to explain yourself. What you should not do is flannel. Come clean. Explain using straightforward words:

> *"I am sorry I am afraid I've lost myself.*
> *Please bear with me."*

Even the most cold-hearted of audiences will give you the benefit of the doubt and allow you time to get yourself together. Make sure you take the time required. Be sure of where you are and only then restart. There is nothing worse than a presentation marred by a series of false starts.

Feedback

The monitoring of feedback, like truth in war, is the first casualty of a presentation that is going wrong. The most obvious feedback is if your audience starts to throw things at you! This is unlikely to happen, but they might start looking at their watches or shuffling their feet.

You will need to watch out for elements of feedback. However, if you have not prepared adequately, you will not have enough brain cells available to you to identify the subtler manifestations of feedback. At worst, this means you can blunder on disastrously, not taking into account the feelings of the audience. As with the other key aspects of presentation, preparation is vital in order to free up as much of your brainpower as possible for the performance elements of your presentation and for the monitoring of feedback. When you start to see an audience looking uncomfortable or shuffling, then you can do something about it on the hoof, by slightly adjusting your presentation to take account of audience response.

Dealing with Interruptions

The worst kind of interruption falls into the category of what is generally described as heckling. Hecklers usually direct their fire at politicians and there are many who say that such individuals deserve all they get. However, skilled politicians know how to deal with hecklers and can often turn them to their advantage. I once witnessed former UK Prime Minister Harold Wilson put down a member of the audience who kept interrupting his speech with shouts of, "Rubbish!" After four or five such interruptions, which up to that point Wilson had studiously ignored, he turned to his adversary as yet again he shouted out, "Rubbish!", and fixed him with a baleful eye.

The Prime Minister had had enough.

"We'll come to your subject in a moment," said Wilson, in his unmistakable northern accent, silencing the heckler once and for all and bringing peals of laughter from the rest of the audience, which only added to the discomfort of the heckler.

Sometimes, when things are going really badly and you have a particularly hostile audience, interruptions can come in the form of missiles. Traditionally, rotten tomatoes and soft fruit serve as suitable projectiles, but for the seasoned heckler any sort of vegetable will do. Winston Churchill was once in full flow on the hustings during an election campaign when up onto the platform bounced a cabbage. Churchill paused and watched the vegetable roll to his feet. He looked in a most deliberate manner first at the audience and then at the cabbage, and then again at the audience, saying,

> "I thought I made it perfectly clear that no one, but no one, was to lose his head!"

Remember that hecklers often do not represent the general body of opinion within the room. True, some in the audience might find a heckler's antics amusing, but most will more likely than not be on your side. After a while, even the wittiest of hecklers can become tedious to even the most ribald of audiences. A good strategy is to throw yourself on the mercy of the audience. Even some of the most powerful speakers know that swallowing your pride and appealing to the better nature of the audience can pay huge dividends.

CASE STUDY — MARGARET THATCHER

Anticipating hecklers — mirroring the audience

In the late 1980s, former UK Conservative Prime Minister, Margaret Thatcher, had been having a pretty torrid time of things and her popularity at that point in her political career was certainly not the highest it had been. She found herself addressing an audience of bankers at dinner in the City of London. Recognising that she was speaking to a group of predominantly white middle class Englishmen, she decided to use a cricketing analogy to confront the issue that no doubt was uppermost in their minds. This is what she said,

"I'm still at the crease, 'though the bowling has been pretty hostile of late. [Laughter] But in case anyone doubted it, let me assure you; there will be no ducking the bouncers, no stonewalling, no playing for time! [More laughter and sustained applause]*"*

It was a perfect way to capture and confront the issue uppermost in the minds of the audience and head off trouble in advance in the unlikely event that there had been a po-tential heckler in the audience.

Key Lesson*: Carefully plan and rehearse what you have to say and be prepared to let your presentation "breathe" as the audience dictates through applause or laughter.*

Once again, proper preparation with good audience analysis is the key to minimising the risks of unwanted interruptions. However, it is vital at all times not to lose sight of reality in your quest to empathise with the target audience. It is very easy to go over the top and sometimes even the best of speakers give an open goal to would-be hecklers. In 1945, when Churchill was trying to win the post-war election, he was in Chatham, one of the naval dockyards which had been crucial to the British war effort. Mindful of the likely occupations of the majority of his audience, he went on at some length about how critical naval activity was to the future of Britain. Unfortunately, he overdid it for one member of the audience, who had clearly had enough when Churchill alluded to his central theme for the umpteenth time, saying,

> "You may be wondering [*Pause*] why do I keep stressing the importance of the Royal Navy? [*Pause, but for just too long*]"

"Because you're in f****** Chatham, that's why!" came a loud and strident voice from the body of the hall.

Churchill survived the interruption and the ensuing laughter of the audience by taking it all in good part with an acknowledging smile recognising that he had gone too far. However, the story goes to show that no one is immune from the predations of hecklers.

How might Churchill have avoided giving such an opportunity to a would-be heckler? Well, he was such a good speaker that he seldom rehearsed and often spoke off-the-cuff without notes. Rehearsal, particularly in front of someone, will often point up potential danger areas and the major minefields can be identified in advance of the presentation proper. Remember that consultation is the key to success and you should not rely on your interpretation alone of the expectations of a given audience. Rehearsal in front of someone can often make a real difference to the way in which your speech is perceived by the audience.

The key element to remember when coping with hecklers is to keep calm. Ignore them if you can. They just might get bored with continuously interrupting and not getting a response, but more likely the rest of the audience will take care of them for you.

If things get too bad, just stop talking. Normally, the audience will go quiet too. Ask them in a neutral manner, but certainly without any hint of annoyance or arrogance, "Would you like me to continue?" If the overwhelming answer comes back, "Yes", then you can legitimately say something like, "Well, perhaps we can keep points and questions until the end."

Of course, if the answer comes back as a resounding "No!" then you would be unwise to continue. There is absolutely no point in trying talk to an audience that simply does not want to listen.

Above all, try to retain your sense of humour. You can only achieve this if you keep your cool. It is far better to "kill" your heckler with politeness than to lower yourself to their level and mix it with them. In the final analysis, it is only a presentation you are giving. It is not a life-and-death matter, and you do not have to win the day on that particular occasion. There will no doubt be other opportunities to get your message across. Far better to stop, make a dignified withdrawal, and regroup for another day.

Having said all the above, I should point out that instances of having to actually stop a presentation are very rare indeed. Most audiences in a business context are polite and restrained. However, do not take the absence of heckling as a sign of the perceived merit of your presentation. Most people these days have perfected the art of looking interested when in reality they may have switched off soon after the opening sentences of your speech. Your presentation can still fail, even if the audience is apparently friendly.

After-dinner Speaking

The occasion when you are most likely to suffer from heckling is the after-dinner speech. The application of large quantities of alcohol to an audience can have a most adverse effect on even the best speakers. I once witnessed one of Britain's best-known comedians struggle with a very well-to-do audience who had attended a prestigious fund-raising charity ball in London held in the presence of royalty. In vain, he attempted to engage their interest with a string of clever and amusing gags, which were his forte. He tried everything but nothing worked. In the end, he was forced to bow out gracefully.

On another occasion, another top performer was the cabaret act at the end of an awards ceremony, which I was chairing. The audience, principally comprised of salespeople, was pretty unruly during my part of the proceedings. By the time the cabaret started, they were totally out of hand. In one part of the thousand-seater room, a bread roll fight had broken out; in another champagne was being sprayed — you can imagine the scene. Those who were not part of the general unruliness were struggling to have a conversation with other members of their table and having to shout to make themselves heard. In short, it was bedlam.

With what they saw as the main purpose of the evening done and dusted, the audience settled down to enjoy themselves in fine style. For the performer, it was a nightmare. He struggled on manfully but after 25 minutes he was forced to cut short his planned 40-minute slot with the memorable words, uttered with not a little sarcasm,

> "Thank you, ladies and gentlemen, for your kind attention. Next year I understand the organisers are arranging a cabaret better suited to your obvious needs — topless darts. Good night!"

The problem is that, once an audience is taken by drink, it is very hard for even the ablest and most talented of performers to bring them back. The best thing you can do is to withdraw gracefully.

If you talk to people arranging dinners at which they have speakers, there is a recurring theme when it comes to fixing speakers. Invariably, they are implored to "keep it short". Of course, most speakers fail to keep to this stricture. Making a short speech is one of the toughest challenges for a presenter. Remember, it was Churchill who said,

> "If you want a long speech, I can have it ready this afternoon. A short speech will take me a couple of days to prepare."

The only way to ensure that a five-minute speech is in fact five minutes is to rehearse it thoroughly. Time is not elastic. Keep to your allotted time and you will be thanked. Overrun and you will be consigned to the dustbin reserved by organisers and audiences alike for people who take up too much time — the one marked "Boring windbags".

Sometimes you will find yourself as one of a series of speakers. If you are at the end of the line and the previous speakers have not only overrun their time but also your own, what do you do? This has happened to me on a number of occasions. I vividly remember being asked to give a vote of thanks to a charity fundraiser who had done extremely well and raised several hundred thousand pounds. I had prepared a glowing speech of fifteen minutes in which I planned to generously blow the trumpet of this wonder fundraiser. I had been told that she would be saying a few words on her retirement from the charity concerned. No one was prepared for what turned out to be a full 45 minutes during which time, with total immodesty, she rattled through all of her achievements. Clearly, this individual wanted to leave nothing to chance.

The audience had already sat through a somewhat over-long and rather tedious concert of obscure chamber music (which was out of keeping with the tastes of the majority of them) and had been kept from eating for 50 per cent longer than the scheduled time. Now they were faced with a speech which overran by 400 per cent! When, to everyone's relief, she finally sat down, what was I to do? Even ten minutes more would have been cruel and unusual punishment to an audience already bored stiff beyond eternity. I decided to keep my remarks to a minimum. I thanked her profusely for her outstanding work and for so comprehensively outlining her achievements and mentioned that, having thus spoken, I would cut my allotted time short. Then, to loud cheers from the audience, I promptly sat down. The lesson to be learnt here is that, if nothing else, ensure that your speech has the merit of brevity!

Before we leave the subject of after-dinner speaking, I should discuss a growing trend, which no doubt is there to cope with the increasing difficulty faced by speakers. Many event organisers are scheduling speakers *before* dinner, perhaps offering a few canapés at the table to stave off any hunger pangs among the diners. This works particularly well when the subject of the speech is serious. It is less easy with a lighter, humorous speech, as seasoned performers will tell you a little alcohol inside the audience serves to loosen up their laughter glands. The trick here is one of balance. There will definitely be a continuing demand for after-dinner speaking which genuinely takes place after dinner, but if possible, especially where you have a serious subject, investigate the possibility of going on before the dinner.

Handling Questions

I always advise that questions are best handled at the end of your presentation. The event is far less messy this way and you will minimise the risk of losing your way in the presentation. You will also be in a far better position to maintain control of the proceedings. There are very few presenters who can take continued interruptions from questioners without being thrown off their stroke. Another reason for taking questions at the end is that, otherwise, you can use up so much of the available time and then not have enough left to complete the presentation. Explain at the beginning of the presentation that you would welcome questions but that you would rather take them at the end.

Depending on the kind of presentation you are doing, you can allow a certain amount of dialogue to develop. If it is a large audience, such as a public meeting or a company AGM, you will want to handle questions in a rather more formal way than in, say, an internal presentation. Here it is much easier to allow a free-flowing discussion to develop. In a formal meeting it is permissible to allow one, possibly two supplementary questions to each individual questioner, but then you must move on. This discipline, even with the most benign of questioners, will help you maintain your authority if the questioning gets tough. Beware too of the long and involved question which gets into very specific detail. The chances are, such questions will turn the rest of the audience off and even if you have made a stunning presentation, the abiding memory the audience will have will be how bored they were by the question-and-answer session. The key here is, as with the presentation itself, to ensure that the questioning has relevance to the majority of the audience.

So what do you do if you find that a questioner is going into too much boring detail? Simply suggest that to answer the question fully would require more time than you have allotted and suggest politely that you will take it up after the meeting. Then move on swiftly to the next question. A suitable form of words might be:

> "Thank you for your question. It is one which I am sure you will appreciate will require some time to answer in detail. What I would like to do is take it up after the meeting. Perhaps you would be kind enough to take it up with me [or indeed a colleague you might depute who would be in a better position to answer the question]. Let's move on to another question."

And with that you turn decisively to another part of the room for another question. This decisive turning to another part of the audience is important, as it has the effect of closing down any further supplementary questions or interruptions from your questioner. It is very hard for them to get back into the action if you are not looking in their direction.

If two or more audience members with opposing points of view begin an argument in the middle of your question-and-answer session, effectively hijacking the presentation, the best thing to do is to interrupt them politely and ask them to continue their discussion afterwards.

As I mentioned above, with internal presentations you can afford to be more relaxed, letting questions range more freely. However, relevance is still the key to successful internal question-and-answer sessions. Do not allow one individual to hog the dialogue at the expense of the others and at the expense of the message which you are trying to get across. It is, however, tough to put this policy into action when the questioning is coming from a superior. I have experienced several instances where a well-prepared and crafted presentation has been hijacked and wrecked by an impatient senior member of the audience. There is no quick fix for this kind of behaviour, save for increasing the recognition of the need for discipline in an audience. This can only be achieved if there is support from

the very top of an organisation. In the absence of such discipline, presenters in a business environment have no alternative but to be philosophical in the face of a barrage of
questioning. After all, as they say in the United States, "It's
their dime!" However, look to yourself. Do you constantly interrupt your direct reports when they are presenting to you?

What If I Do Not Know *the Answer to a Particular Question?*

Inevitably, there will be times when you will be asked a question to which you do not know the answer. If you do not, then
say so. Do not flannel but instead promise to find out the answer and get back to the questioner. Of course, it goes without
saying that you must fulfil your promise. Once you have given
your word, move swiftly on to the next question. Use the following form of words:

> "I'm terribly sorry, but that's a question I haven't been
> asked before and I'm afraid I don't have a ready answer.
> What I will do is try to find out what you want to know
> and come back to you."

What If I Do Not *Want to Answer a Particular Question?*

The more senior a presenter, the more likely it is that they will
have access to information which has to remain confidential.
Sometimes this is for commercial reasons, sometimes for legal
reasons. It is perfectly legitimate for you to say to a questioner
that you are unable to help with an answer to a particular
question; use the phrases discussed in Chapter 2, such as:

> "I'm afraid the answer to that question would mean me
> breaking commercial confidentiality. I hope you will ap-
> preciate I am simply not at liberty to answer that ques-
> tion."

If it is a legal or quasi-legal issue, then say so but try to avoid
Latin legalese such as, "The matter is *sub judice*." So few peo-

ple these days have studied Latin at school that many regard
the use of such phrases as pompous, even though they are in
themselves accurate. Far better to use a more user-friendly
form of words:

> "I am sorry, but the question you ask covers areas that
> are subject to legal discussions. I hope you will appreci-
> ate that I cannot discuss this at the moment."

Wherever possible, try to give hope to the audience about
when you might be able to shed more light on the subject,
thus:

> "We hope for a conclusion to the legal negotiations
> within a week to ten days. We should be able to give you
> more information after that."

Note the use of the words "hope" and "should". Neither com-
mits you to future action and it goes without saying that you
should never lay yourself open by making promises which
could be stymied by the all-too-frequent delay of due legal
process.

You should not be apologetic about being unable to answer
a given question if you have good grounds for not doing so.
During the Gulf War against Saddam Hussein's Iraq in the
early 1990s, a very sure-footed American colonel was handling
one of the daily press conferences.

He was being asked a series of questions about allied troop
movements. All were parried deftly, but with little real detail,
all of which proved rather frustrating for the journalists, one
of whom decided to be rather more direct:

"Colonel, could you be more specific about the precise nature of the troop movements?"

"No, Sir!"

"But Colonel, why not?"

"Because I don't want to," riposted the Colonel with an air of finality.

Of course, the military spokesman has might on his side and, in this case, also right, as there was no way he wanted to jeopardise the safety of soldiers on the ground. In the face of such moral high ground, it is a very bold questioner indeed who will press their case.

Remember the Big Finish

When either time or the questions have run out, it is tempting to allow the presentation to fizzle out — a kind of "Er . . . that's it . . ." approach. This tends to leave your audience rather flat. All good performers know that you have to leave your audience on a high note. So remember to sum up for a minute or two. Thank the audience for their questions — celebrating the calibre of such questions. Quickly summarise the key points of your original presentation and — a crucial point this — repeat the call to action. Tell them once again what you expect them to do.

Key Points to Remember

- You must "break the ice" with the audience from the start.

- Your opening should say, "Hey, guess what?"

- Smile.

- Use eye contact.

- If you are nervous and find yourself shaking, consciously try to control your twitching.

- Use your breathing to keep calm and paced.

- Organise your prompt cards in two piles; be prompted from the left-hand card, moving the right-hand one gradually across when you are finished.

- If you are to use Autocue, make sure you are completely familiar with its operations.

- If you dry, take stock and look at your prompt cards. When you are sure of yourself, look up and start again.

- Monitor audience feedback and reaction throughout your speech.

- Anticipate hecklers and interruptions by preparing well and knowing your audience's expectations.

- Do not get carried away in your efforts to empathise with the audience.

- Keep questions until the end.

- Keep your cool at all times.

- Do not overrun your allotted time.

- If previous speakers have overrun, cut your speech short.

- If you do not know the answer to a question, then say so.

- If you do not *want* to answer a particular question, then say why.

- Thank the audience for their questions.

- Quickly summarise your key points and repeat the call to action.

PART TWO
External Presentations

Chapter 6

THE CREDENTIALS PRESENTATION

Up to now we have dealt with what can be described as generic presentations. Despite the availability of faster electronic means of communication, increasingly in business life people seek face-to-face communication with potential customers. Only with such contact do you have the opportunity of spelling out in person what you have to offer. And of course, if you are a good communicator you can do this with an impact and passion that would otherwise be hard to achieve with a written or telephoned communication.

A Changing Environment

These days, all serious corporations have accountants, bankers, lawyers, PR companies, etc. in place, so the chances of making an instant sale are relatively rare. However, many corporations see it as their duty from time to time to review their incumbent suppliers, whether it is of product or professional services. In this way, they can at the very least stay alive to what else is potentially available to them in the marketplace.

For this reason, a great deal of activity goes on in the field of what has commonly become known as the "Credentials Presentation". Some companies have laid down review policies whereby they will examine suppliers on a regular basis. Sometimes there is a prescribed cycle — for example, once every three years for PR companies, every five years for accountants and other professionals. Often, companies are rather more *ad hoc* in the way they cast about for alternative suppliers. There is never a right time to make a credentials presentation to these sort of companies and the success or failure of a presentation can be very much a hit-and-miss affair.

There have been changes in the marketplace too. Generally speaking, in recent years companies are much more ready to chop and change suppliers with, in many cases, traditional concepts of loyalty going out the window. However, some larger, better-managed companies have been going through exercises in what is known as supply chain reduction. This usually means cutting down the numbers of suppliers and placing more orders in the hands of a few. My own company recently went through a process with one customer who decided to reduce the number of training suppliers from over 1,000 to less than 20. Fortunately, we were one of the survivors!

Some professions — law for example — appear to have lost forever the once traditional expectation that all professional work for a given client should be placed with them. Such one-stop-shop monopoly has gone in the face of growing complexity and specialisation within the legal profession. Today, the client is much more likely to exercise choice on a case-by-case basis, with one law firm being used for commercial conveyancing and another for, say, intellectual property work.

In accountancy, changes in standards and in some cases the law has meant a loss of client monopoly too. Whilst one firm may take on the audit of a client company, they may find themselves proscribed from offering, for example, tax advice. This can create tensions where audit work has become almost a commodity product in accountancy, and as such provides relatively lowly rewards, with other disciplines in the professions such as corporate finance and tax advice being much more lucrative. This has led today to more than one account-ant seriously asking the question, "Who would be an auditor?"

So, all in all the marketplace has become much more chal-lenging, but with that challenge have come many more opportunities which can be exploited through competent pres-entation. Such opportunities have a much better chance of becoming business realities if presentation invitations are taken seriously and seized with both hands. From the very start, all such invitations should be treated as sales opportu-nities, no matter how entrenched the incumbent supplier ap-pears to be.

Over-reliance on Branding

So often when one organisation presents to another, the pre-senters over-rely on the "brand value" of their firm. You see this particularly with the big banking institutions and with professional firms of accountants and lawyers. Millions are invested in branding. One of the biggest costs in mergers of professional firms is the rebranding of the newly merged en-tity. In 1998, the merger of Price Waterhouse and Coopers & Lybrand into PricewaterhouseCoopers resulted, among other things, in the creation of a range of "branded" colours. Only these colours could be used in the new firm for everything from printed material to large format banners at seminars and presentations. Branding is an important element of the mar-keting activity of any modern business.

It is widely held that it is the brand that gets you through the door. This is true, but that is all that the brand does on its own. After that, you have to make the running on your own. This is where so many people presenting on behalf of famous brands fall down. There is already tremendous expectation built up in the minds of the audience. When you make a pres-entation, to be successful you must marshal some of the key elements of branding and advertising. And this must run through the entire presentation, even down to the language you use. Essentially, you want to "enshrine" the values of your brand in your presentation. What do we mean by this? Well it is all a question of ensuring that what you say you are going to do is delivered in such away that it matches your brand values. No doubt, you will want to be thought of as open, honest, efficient, straightforward, totally free of any complication or pomposity. These are laudatory aspirational values for any brand. They must be reflected in your presentation, so use simple language rather than complicated, overblown constructions. Say what you can do, and say it passionately, because the audience must believe that you believe, without you sounding grand or overbearing. Above all, you must be honest and must never say you will do something unless you have the ability to deliver and the will to carry it through. In essence, you are packaging yourself as a brand: wrapping yourself in the flag of your brand.

Brand values are all about the benefits that will accrue to the purchaser of a particular brand. Advertisers know this very well. For example, the picture on a tin of dog food is invariably one of a happy, healthy dog. This of course does not mean that inside the can is chopped up dog. What the can is trying to portray is the benefit that your dog will get through eating this food. Similarly, if you buy a box of grass seed, the picture on the box is not a picture of grass seed but a picture of what you get as a result of sowing this seed — a lush, green sward stretching out in beautiful, even stripes.

This focus on brand values has been keenly pursued by some companies for over a century. Some companies have grown in respect and prosperity as a result of this attention to brand value. Everybody knows what a can of Heinz baked beans looks like. Turquoise and black is the colour scheme. In the supermarket, even from a distance out of the corner of your eye, you are immediately drawn to the Heinz can. Those colours enshrine the brand values, the taste, quality, and integrity of the product. The brand therefore makes you an offer. In exchange, you are prepared to pay a premium price for these brand values. Brands, built up over several years, nurtured, enhanced and protected, can stand the test of intense competition. In the 1990s, Heinz faced an onslaught from supermarkets' "B" brands, offered to the public at as little as a few pence per can compared to the Heinz price of 39 pence. The premium brand weathered the storm remarkably well. The bean-eating public trusted their familiar brand and the brand stood up well.

It takes time to build brand values and sometimes the brand-building is far from straightforward, even for well-established brands, particularly when trying to break into established markets. When in the mid-1990s Heinz started to introduce baked beans to the new republic of Russia, they realised they could not rely on the famous turquoise. They were forced to use pictures of the beans on the outside of the can, because Russians were not familiar with the product. No doubt in the fullness of time they will evolve this brand to become consistent with the Heinz colour scheme throughout the world.

The Nature of the Credentials Presentation

In a way, the credentials presentation is a misnomer because it gives the impression to the presenting team that somehow this is not a sales opportunity but simply a rather cosy get-together for a chat over tea and buns. Where there is an opportunity to mention gently what your firm can do at some future misty date, should the remote opportunity arise, it is a bonus. The reality is that every presentation opportunity dubbed a credentials presentation is potentially a chance to sell. For this reason, these days credentials presentations have to be much more effective than they used to be.

Such is the pace of corporate life that everyone's time is precious. If you can add value to your audience's business through your credentials presentation, in such a way that the audience feels they have received some kind of extra wisdom as a result of seeing you, then you may be on your way to replacing the current incumbents in your particular discipline. In other words, as with all presentations, relevance is the watchword and you will have to tailor each and every credentials presentation to the specific prospect each time.

It is of little use, for example, for a bank which boasts a sophisticated retail branch network, with a branch in every UK High Street, to emphasise this fact if the prospect is London-based and conducts most of its work overseas. You might think that no organisation would be that stupid. Sadly, the reality is quite different and we have witnessed many firms falling into just that trap. This is principally due to the tyranny of the so-called "Standard Credentials Presentation".

The Standard Credentials Presentation

Standard Credentials Presentations are created by firms for the best possible of motives. Senior management wants to ensure that more junior presenters give consistent messages to outsiders about the activities of their firm. They also want to help those who are less experienced get through what is often a most daunting experience, remembering that eight out of ten people in business find making a presentation the most daunting thing they have to do in business life. So why not remove some of the pain by spoon-feeding them a prepared credentials presentation?

Clearly, there is underlying good sense in creating some kind of standard credentials presentation, and we have helped many organisations work up such templates. Interestingly, these exercises can often serve to help an organisation sort out what it is it really stands for and just what are the key features and benefits it offers. Whilst most people in an organisation will feel they have a good grasp of their firm's principles of business, invariably the process highlights differences of perception between senior members of a firm about such issues. Having to articulate the pluses and minuses of a firm's operations forces individuals in a management team to confront issues and tensions. The process of putting order on these issues helps iron them out and organise them into some kind of cogent message that everyone in the organisation can stand behind.

We call such a process an exercise in "singing off the same hymn sheet". Sometimes we discover that not only are members of a management team not singing off the same hymn sheet, they are often not in the same church and occasionally not even of the same religion! This is a classic example of how preparation of a presentation can act as a powerful management tool for change. Even when there are fundamental differences of opinion over a wide range of issues, the discipline of having to rationalise the arguments into clear and concise messages can have a profound impact on management. There is almost a cathartic effect which comes about through everyone, as it were, having their blood spilled on the carpet at the same time, but coming through the process with a much greater sense of togetherness.

So standard credentials presentations are useful and they do have their place in any organisation, if only to help them sort out and articulate the true messages they wish to promote to the outside world. However, I am always at pains to point out that such prepared standard presentations should be used only as, if you like, the backbone or core to any presentation, rather than as a generic representation of all that is good and powerful in a given organisation. I am aware that this advice flies in the face of many who see the chief advantage of a set credentials presentation as ensuring consistency of approach and message, no matter who puts it across. Whilst this is a justifiable aim, the chief disadvantage is that it can very quickly become stale and dated and be seen as such by any prospects, because it appears to be a "one-size-fits-all" presentation. Also, as we have already mentioned, if a bald standard credentials presentation is made come what may, you will risk turning off your audience by including information which has no bearing on their needs.

Another issue surrounding the standard credentials presenation is one of shelf life. Most companies treat standard credentials presentation as almost permanent documents. Rather like generic company brochures, they are written once (such creativity being generally regarded as a chore) and then forgotten until a really major change in the company's activities dictates a review of the material. More usually, the brochure is reviewed only when the print order has run out and even then it is much easier to order a reprint from the old plates.

With credentials presentations, thanks in part to electronic slide production, it is easier to make changes and we would recommend a review on a regular basis, say once every six months. It almost goes without saying that the updated presentation should then be circulated to all those involved with presenting the firm's credentials, together with the reasons underlying any changes that have been made. It is a good idea too to ensure that presenters retain "battle fitness" for presentations. We run update "clinics" for clients, where individual presenters can come along for an hour and update their skills. Even seasoned presenters with high levels of intrinsic and developed skills find value in such update tutorials and often amaze themselves when they see how many bad habits they may have slipped into.

Tailoring your Presentation

I have already established that to be really effective a credentials presentation has to have some elements of tailoring to it. That is to say, it must appear to the audience as something that has been put together with that particular audience very much in mind. Many an opportunity has been lost because an otherwise very polished and professional presentation has fallen wide of the mark, having ignored key elements of what the particular audience was expecting to hear.

One of the most basic ways of tailoring a credentials presentation, and one which is frequently observed these days, is that of simply putting the prospect's logo on the title slide. Whilst this is laudable, it runs the risk of also being laughable if that is the only element of tailoring that goes into the presentation. Much better to demonstrate in the presentation that you know something of the prospect's business and have clearly thought about which particular aspects of your operations will provide solutions to the problems and needs of the prospect.

These days, a visit to their web site is a must for every member of the presentation team. Indeed, in the planning stages of the presentation, it would be worth picking out one or two issues that you believe are pertinent to the prospect and focusing on how your operation could be of service to them in these areas. In our own business, we make it a rule to add half a dozen pertinent printed-out pages from a prospect's web site to the documentation our consultants carry with them when meeting a prospect for the first time. It is amazing how useful such a printout can be when reviewed just prior to the presentation. Even though such meetings would be judged by many as falling into the category of "informal, across the table" encounters, we regard them all as presentation events and selling opportunities at that.

Typically, most unschooled credentials presentations focus far too heavily on the history and development of the presenting organisation. It still amazes me how well-established businesses boasting household brand names, whether they be in the field of fast-moving consumer goods or in something less tangible such as banking, still feel the need to trot out all sorts of historical information about themselves. While of great interest to those working for the organisation itself, it is probably of little relevance to the prospect. Nonetheless, many credentials presentations start off with yards and yards of history rather than offering clear, up-front headlines spelling out what might be in it for the prospect. Much better to keep all the historical stuff to a bare minimum — certainly no more than five per cent of the presentation as a whole. Give a small amount of relevant history near the start and then quickly move into the areas where you can establish how the services of your organisation can really benefit your prospect.

Look out too for gratuitous information which is more "plate polishing" and aggrandising to the presenting organisation. Do a 180-degree assessment of your material and ask yourself honestly how you would feel about the bolder statements in your current credentials. Not that it is bad to be bold, in as much you will fare far better if you are positive in what you say, but you must also look out for the negative connotations which might attach themselves to certain seemingly positive assertions. Among such statements might be, "We think you will want to hire us because we are the biggest." Well they might, but they also might feel that being so large you might not be able to give them as personal and committed a service as a smaller provider in the same field. For most people, size is important, but the issue of size might read differently to different audiences.

Remember the campaign waged by Avis against their arch-rivals and leaders in the hire car sector, Hertz. Avis made a

virtue of being runner-up. Whilst Hertz understandably ma-
jored on their pole position be trumpeting that they were
Number 1, Avis took every opportunity to stress the effort they
were making because of their second place. The slogan "We try
harder" was born and was to run successfully for decades.

Putting Together the Right Team

Most credentials presentations are carried out by teams. Often, these teams are thrown together at very short notice and
comprise disparate team members drawn from the far reaches
of the organisation. It is quite usual in large professional organisations for team members never to have met before. Such
a hurried coming-together of individuals requires strict adher-
ence to the basic rules of team presentations if the opportunity is to have any hope of success.

First and foremost, a team has to have a leader. Even if it is
a team of two, one person should clearly be in charge. The
leader's job is to chair the event and maintain control — control of the team and — an important point — control of the
audience. This is essential at all stages but it is particularly
critical during the question-and-answer sessions that are so
much an everyday part of modern business presentations. A
good leader or team chairman who is clearly in control often
finds it possible to buy time during question-and-answer sessions, by repeating a question or seeking clarification. This
ensures that each question can be adequately and cogently
answered. It also lessens the possibility of a member of the
team being left floundering when trying to instantly answer a
question "on the hoof".

Whilst it is important for the leader to be clearly in charge
of proceedings, it is vital that he or she is not perceived as
dominating the presentation. This is often difficult, as the
leader will generally be the most experienced and knowledge-
able of those present. He is also likely to be the most senior.

There is a fine line to tread between being in charge and dominating a presentation. However, a really successful chairman should adopt a role rather more akin to the conductor of the orchestra than the soloist, bringing in the other presenters and helping make them look good.

Here is an important point. What customers and clients are looking for is continuity and consistency of approach from any supplier. They will be concerned if there is a huge discrepancy between the perceived abilities of one member of the team (usually the chairman) and some of the others. You will need to field a balanced team. If there is a difference between the presentational skills of the best and the worst, it will not help the prospects of success. Most prospects understand that it cannot be the team leader alone who delivers the service in the long term. However, they expect a discernible level of competence from all team members. It is critical, therefore, that the leader ensures that the others, who may well be more involved with the day-to-day delivery of service, are allowed to shine.

To do this well requires a correct mix in the presentation team. In many service industries and the professions, it is often the senior people, partners and directors, who are the best presenters. Their very position depends not so much on their ability but on their "clubability" — the ease with which they can mix with new people across a wide spectrum and strike up a persuasive relationship with them in a relatively short space of time.

Some years ago, we were working with a large firm of accountants. It was during the mid-1980s, a time of high growth in the accountancy world. The particular office with which we were working needed to add four new partners rapidly to cope with the growth in their business. The problem was where to find such talent. As the accountancy sector as a whole was experiencing a shortage of good people to fuel heightened demand, finding new partners externally was going to be tough.

The existing partners in the office were not at all convinced there were the necessary skills within the practice to fill the partner positions internally. One of the key perceived issues was the poor communications skills of rising accountancy managers, which is why we were called.

We uncovered a fundamental conundrum of technically based businesses. In the early career stages, technical ability is what gets you noticed and fuels your progress. The problem is, to be a partner requires a whole new set of skills that are often antipathetic to the core skills, and indeed inclinations, of these young technocrats. In short, the majority of young graduates who opted for professions such as accountancy, law or banking did so on the basis that they would not have to sell anything to anyone.

The partners in this particular case felt there was no promotable talent to fill the new partner shortage. However, presentational and clubability talent is often hard to spot. We implemented an exercise which combined presentations skills tutorials with development and talent spotting. At the end of the programme, we identified, from a cadre of 40 young qualified accountants, six who we believed had the potential to make partner, four of whom actually did so within the next 18 months.

The whole issue of the gap between technical ability and the ability to present well is particularly thrown into sharp focus when one looks, for example, at how public relations companies traditionally dealt with competitive pitches (until the more enlightened ones improved their act in the mid-1990s). Typically when trying to win business, PR companies would front up with their very senior people plus the designated account executive, who would be much more junior and invariably with poorly developed presentation skills. Invariably, Mr High Powered (it was invariably a man in this role) would do most of the talking, only occasionally bringing in other team members (usually female) to add what he might have regarded as their "fluffy" embellishments to his lordly words of wisdom. The PR world was not too keen on the image portrayed by TV programmes such as *Absolutely Fabulous*, but as with all such programmes, there was a grain of truth in the scripting.

Certainly the clients did not like the old-style approach to such presentations. Many have told us how they did not take kindly to being persuaded and convinced by an individual whom they subsequently hardly saw again. It is for this reason that PR companies to this day are dogged by the same question when they go to present their credentials: "Who is actually going to handle the account?" That individual should be allowed to speak and thus should have the ability to speak ably and succinctly on the subject. If they are unable to speak effectively, then they must be given training and help in order to do this.

Ensuring that the entire team is up to scratch presentationally is easy to say and far harder to put into practice. Take, for example, a manufacturing company supplying components for the car industry. Its products are such that a potential purchaser will want to be sure that the right people are in place to deliver the products regularly and to a consistently high quality. Assurances from the Managing Director will of course be essential, but how much better if, as part if the credentials presentation, you include the Production Director? Audiences like to see the whites of the eyes of such individuals and to get their personal assurances that "Just-in-Time" will mean just that and not just too late. Similarly, when it comes to quality, they will want to see that this concept is ingrained throughout the operations of the potential supplier and not just fine thoughts in the mind of one or two directors.

By selecting the right team, you can ensure that your credentials presentation has a greater chance of being remembered. That is the chief aim of such presentations, for often the timing is not ideal in terms of the real needs of the prospect organisation. As we said earlier, most organisations have incumbent suppliers in all major roles. If you are invited to make a credentials presentation, you have to use the opportunity to plant thoughts in the minds of your audience which might stir them to believe they have need of your organisation. If you can turn those thoughts of need into real wants and real desires, then your ordinary credentials presentations will easily take on the mantle of full-blown sales presentations; but do so in a subtle manner. The acid test is of course whether you win new business. Such occurrences, while rare, do happen and you need to be alive to them as possibilities.

From Credentials Presentation to Sales Pitch

One reason for the credentials presentation to turn into a live sales opportunity is a change of circumstance for the prospect. There can often be a delay of several weeks between the booking of the appointment and the delivery of the presentation. If a week is famously a "long time in politics", it can be a time of significantly change in the world of business. On a number of occasions, my colleagues and I have been to what we had anticipated to be a fairly low-key information-gathering meeting. We had expected to lay out our stall with a credentials presentation tailored to the researched needs of the prospect. What of course is hard to glean from desk research is the current state of need within a prospect organisation. On numerous occasions over the years, we have arrived at a prospect only to find a particular live need that needs a solution only our company can provide.

One obvious sign of this is the inclusion of an extra, unannounced meeting participant. Sometimes, such individuals are introduced with little more than, "Mr So-and-so will just sit in at our meeting. I hope you don't mind." Mr So-and-so is bound to be a busy man, so he is usually sitting in because he has a real and immediate need. He is not disclosing his hand, because he wants to see you perform before committing himself. Even though you are all prepared with a presentation, take time to probe gently about Mr So-and-so's position. Quite often, he will be a new appointee to the company charged with a particular task. Even though he is in fact-finding mode, this is your opportunity to strike. For him, despite incumbent suppliers, newness is a positive asset — it gives him a chance to make his mark. The ability to move swiftly up a gear and switch into sales mode is key in such situations. Adaptability is crucial. You should seek feedback from this person to find out where their interests lie. Clearly, what you must not do is insist on ploughing on with your planned credentials presentation, ignoring obvious "buy" signals from the prospect. As ever, the watchword is flexibility.

Key Points to Remember

- A credentials presentation should always be treated as an opportunity to create sales.

- Keep in mind the brand values of your organisation, but do not over-rely on these.

- Use the preparation of standard credentials presentations to highlight differences of perception between senior members of a firm about what is important in the organisation.

- Standard credentials presentations should be used only as a backbone to any presentation, which should then always be tailored to the needs of each audience.

- Review your standard credentials presentation regularly.

- As in all presentations, offer clear up-front headlines emphasising what's in it for the prospect.

- Research the prospect company well in advance, and show in your presentation that you know what they want.

- Select a balanced team with a good leader and strong back-up.

- Be wary of changed circumstances for the prospect company, which might alter your chances of success for better or worse.

- Stay alert for obvious "buy" signals from the prospect.

- Be flexible.

Chapter 7

THE SALES PRESENTATION

Sales presentations or direct pitches for business differ from credentials presentations inasmuch as they focus on specific sales opportunities. Often such opportunities will have arisen from a credentials presentation. It may well be that several months have elapsed since the original presentation and now the prospect has come back to you and asked you to present on a specific business proposition. Although the proposition may be specific in the mind of the prospective client, you may find that it is often less well-defined than you would like. Indeed, when making sales presentations, the proposition can range from a very tightly defined tender through to a vaguely worded "what if" invitation to pitch.

Expectations

Sometimes clients are purposely vague in the hope that the various pitches will help clarify their thinking. Certainly some firms are brazen in their use of competitive pitching in order to seek ideas and obtain advice on the cheap. In other instances, suppliers are invited to pitch at far too early a stage in the formulation of the prospect's plans, simply because of lack of experience in the prospect team.

Clearly the first issue facing you as the potential supplier is to define exactly what it is you are pitching for. Wherever possible, try to gather information directly from the client in advance of the presentation. During this fact-finding process,

you should attempt to clarify and refine precisely what the expectations of the client are, bearing in mind that these may be
constantly changing. Do not assume that the content of the
original invitation to pitch will necessarily bear any relation to
the expectations of the audience on the day of the pitch
proper. Frequently you will find yourself pitching to individuals with whom you have had no prior contact. When pitching
to such individuals, remember the golden rule:

> *Do not underestimate their intelligence*
> *but do not overestimate their knowledge.*

Be prepared to spell out the fundamentals about your business, even at the expense of going over old ground already
covered with the gatekeepers of the prospect firm.

Sometimes pitching companies are unsure of the correctness of seeking clarification in advance of the pitch, particularly when the presentation is part of a formal tendering
process. Certainly it is true that some organisations are very
strict about having no prior contact with pitch teams, citing
the need to be scrupulously fair to all those pitching. However,
some prospective clients will positively welcome and appreciate any attempt to provide a more focused proposal through
advance dialogue between their project managers and a prospective pitch team. Obviously, you will have to tread carefully
until you have established precisely the attitude of the prospect towards such approaches, but fear of rejection is no excuse for not attempting to gain advance information which will
help you prepare a more polished presentation.

The importance of understanding how quickly circumstances can change in the time between the original request
for a proposal to the day of the pitch itself cannot be overesti-
mated. My own firm, having conducted considerable advance
intelligence work, turned up at a leading financial services
company to make a presentation for what we were assured

was a significant amount of business. We had been in communication over several weeks with senior managers in charge of training within the prospect organisation. Now we were to pitch to eight managing directors responsible for the key divisions within the prospect firm. We were to be the last of three companies pitching for the business. Our pitch team comprised myself and two colleagues. We had carefully honed and rehearsed our presentation (naturally!), paying close attention to the various modifications to the brief which had been fed to us by our contacts within the target firm.

When we arrived at their swish premises in the City of London, we were met by rather embarrassed training managers. Having seen the other two pitches the previous afternoon, the MDs had decided that the brief was all wrong and they unanimously decided there and then to shelve their training plans. The MDs were busy people, so did not feel there was any point in seeing anyone else, as they were not going to go ahead with further development at that stage. Our journey had been wasted. For us, it represented many man-hours of work down the drain. What a horror story! Clearly, there was little we could have done to cope with such a dramatic turn-around. We had fallen foul of internal politics and it is hard to imagine what we could have done to avoid such an outcome. However, the example goes to show how quickly circumstances can change.

Notwithstanding how much communication has been achieved over and above the basic request for a proposal, it is vital in your preparation to ensure that the presentation ties in as precisely as possible with the proposition being put forward by the client. If you are responding to a tender, this should be a relatively easy process. You will no doubt have already submitted a written tender response. The main issue to remember here is not to attempt in your spoken presentation to repeat the detail that is contained in your written tender document. What you should do instead is pull out the key points, including costs, and imbue them with your passion and enthusiasm for winning the business. If you have been able to flesh out the original tender document with additional information gained from talking to the prospect team, then it is important to reflect this in your presentation.

Remember, there may be people in your audience, such as non-executive directors, who will not know that you have had extra information. They will probably only have the official tender document as their base information. What is needed is for you to signpost in your presentation elements that reflect your conversations with the prospect, as opposed to the written official document itself. Critical here is openness. You should use phrases such as:

> "We appreciate, having spoken to some of your people, that what you are really looking for here is . . ."

Although you should be open about the fact that you have had contact with the prospect, over and above the official channels, you may feel it appropriate not to name names in case that puts an individual on the spot. Also, you should not give an impression that you have in any way struck up a special or cosy relationship with any individual member of the prospective client firm. It is important not to convey the impression that in some way you consider you have an "inside track". If you do, you will embarrass any individuals with whom you have had contact if they are present in the audience. Even if they are not present, you may cause problems for them with their superiors and you certainly run the risk of putting the backs of the key decision-makers up.

Where you are dealing with complicated proposals, whether in response to formal tender requests or less formal general pitches, there is a great temptation to become absorbed in the process of preparation, responding line-by-line to the request.

This is of course what is required but if you are not careful, when it comes to the pitch itself, you run the risk of being perceived as mechanistic and dull.

Once you have finalised what it is you want to say, you should use rehearsals to reinvigorate your performance so that you put the sizzle back into your presentation. There is a great risk that, in getting too involved in your presentation, you end up boring yourself with it and therefore sounding boring! A golden rule in sales presentations is that you must indicate your keenness to have the business. I have seen so many cases where people have failed to win pitches because they have been less than enthusiastic and turned in what can only be described as a plodding presentation.

Getting the Pitch Team Right

Whilst the credentials presentation may have involved senior members of your organisation, it is critical that in a sales presentation you field the team that is actually going to carry through the work being proposed. This is particularly important in the field of professional services. A recurring criticism from clients is that the urbane and avuncular "grey hairs" turn up and dominate the pitch and if successful are never seen again once the business has been landed. It is important, therefore, that all members of the team are given a role, no matter how much better the team leader might be at presentation. It is important also that, even if the pitch is to be "conducted" by a senior grey hair, the person nominated to be project leader is allowed to shine. The key here is to raise the game of each member of the team so that they put forward their commitment to the prospective client in a high level manner.

The Question-and-Answer Session

Inevitably, when pitching for a specific piece of business, your prospective clients will want to ask questions. Ideally, it would be better to allow two-thirds of the available time, if not more, for questions and answers. Of course, the prospective client will have their own ideas about this. Some of the better organised ones will have thought this through in advance and may even have spelled out, for example, that they will be allowing 45 minutes for the presentation — 15 minutes for your pitch and half an hour of questions and answers. By allowing what appears to be an excessive amount of time for questions, you can avoid a number of pitfalls. Firstly, you can lessen the risk of covering issues in which the prospective client is not interested. Secondly, you can avoid the prospect of not covering a particular issue that was very high on the client's agenda. Thirdly, the question-and-answer session allows you to develop themes which are of particular significance to the prospect and, most importantly, at both the request and the pace of the client. Above all, and this is particularly true where there has been no informal fact-finding contact with the prospect, it give you a better chance of converting the pitch to a sale by fact-finding "on the hoof" and adjusting your pitch accordingly.

It is critical that you identify the decision-making unit — that is, those people who are critical to you getting the business. Again, this is something which ideally should be done in advance of the presentation. If you are unable to do this, then it is vital that you stay alert in the early stages of the pitch to ensure that you direct key points to the appropriate people in your audience.

It is said that all good selling is done by listening. Listen carefully to the questions. Remember to pause before answering them. There is nothing more infuriating than having someone "gap searching" — that is, looking for a gap in which to jump in with a quick answer even before the questioner has finished speaking. Make sure you listen attentively to the questions, making notes as you go if the question is long and involved. A studious pause before you answer will give added impact and gravitas to what you subsequently have to say in response.

Rehearsing likely questions is as important as rehearsing the pitch itself. Get your pitch team together and make the presentation to colleagues, asking them to play the role of the prospective client and fire at you the most awkward and searching questions they can think of. Usually, these questions, because the questioners have a far deeper knowledge of your firm than any client, are much tougher than you will actually encounter on the day. If you can handle such questioning, you will perform even better when you are questioned by the client.

Remember that the team has to have discipline when answering questions. It should not be a free-for-all. The question-and-answer session is a good opportunity for the pitch team to display its cohesiveness. The team should demonstrate "followship" and defer to the pitch team leader before jumping in with an answer. Sometimes you will not have a ready answer to a question. If this is the case, say so, do not waffle. Promise to come back to the inquirer with an answer at a later stage. In any event, it is a good idea to have one of your team actually noting down all the questions so that, if need be, they can be addressed after the presentation through a follow-up letter.

It is useful when answering questions to follow up your answer with a supplementary question along the lines of "Does that cover what you had in mind?" or even better, "Could we suggest another approach to this particular issue?" Anything you can do to soften the edges of what starts off inevitably as a confrontational exercise and turn it into a more consensual and almost collegiate approach will pay dividends in terms of increasing the likelihood of turning the pitch into a sale.

Even before you get to the question-and-answer session, there may of course be objections and interruptions. It goes without saying that each issue raised should be dealt with courteously and with no hint of impatience or tetchiness. If you are unable to come up with an answer instantly to an objection or point that is made, then acknowledge this fulsomely and offer to come back to the questioner with an answer once you've had an opportunity to investigate the issue further.

Closing Your Pitch

Towards the end of the session, it is perfectly legitimate to ask what the next steps might be. A good question is, "When might you be making your decision?" If possible, get them to put a time frame on the whole process, adding that you would like to be able to plan the particular piece of work into your diary. They should be understanding of this and will see such a request as nothing more than a simple but professional approach.

If possible, take an opportunity at the end of the questions to restate in four or five sentences the key reasons why you think you should have the business, again imbuing what you say with passion, conviction and commitment.

Finally, when you have made your presentation, do not forget to follow it up with a letter thanking the organisation for their time and also covering any points which you were unable to answer directly during the question-and-answer session.

Key Points to Remember

- Try to get as much information as possible from the client before the presentation.

- Always show your keenness to have the prospect's business.

- Choose the appropriate people for the presenting team.

- Allow two-thirds of the time for questions and answers.

- Rehearse likely questions.

- Establish a clear time frame for placing the business.

- Summarise your key selling points at the end of the session.

- Follow up with a letter of thanks, clarifying any points where necessary.

Chapter 8

PRESENTING TO BANKERS AND FINANCIERS (1): RAISING FINANCE

Presentations to bankers and financiers fall into two broad categories. The first is to raise the initial money for a business venture; the second is to report progress and ensure that your financial support remains in place and indeed, where appropriate, that you have paved the way to raising further funds should they be required. The first category is discussed in this chapter; the second is discussed in Chapter 9.

We already know and understand the need in any presentation to take into account the expectations of the audience. When it comes to raising money, and indeed when it comes to talking to bankers for whatever reason, this principle is fundamental. The banker is looking for a number of things. First of all, they will want to obtain enough information to be able to make a real assessment of the risks involved. They will want to get a feel for the size and shape of the deal. They will want, in effect, to price the deal in terms of the time and effort involved in carrying it through and to gauge the likely rewards their financial institution can expect if the deal comes off. This way, they can understand whether the deal is for them and the particular financial facilities they have under their care. If the deal is a large one, they will want to make preparations to syndicate the capital involved to other financial institutions and thus spread the risk. Even if the deal is relatively small and well within the capacity of their own institution, the banker will invariably want to consult with colleagues. This means that, particularly when raising money, you have to be prepared to talk to a number of people from the same organisation and often on a number of occasions.

So it is worth bearing in mind that banking decisions always involve a number of individuals within the organisation and beyond if the deal is bigger than one institution can handle. From the point of view of the prospective borrower, this is tedious but unavoidable. However, banks are increasingly recognising that it can be irksome to business people with an entrepreneurial spirit to have to explain themselves over and over because no one individual has the clout to take things forward and they are more sensitive to this frustration, but it still remains a necessity.

Usually investment bankers are running with a number of deals at once. They are under enormous time pressure and they simply may not have had a chance to fill in their colleagues with anything but the briefest of details about your proposal. It is wise therefore to approach each presentation to a new bank official on the basis that the new audience, although from the same organisation, knows nothing about you and your proposition. If you are unsure of just how much they might know, a good ploy is to ask permission of the audience to recite some of the basic details about the deal. Even if there are those listening who may have heard earlier presentations, it does no harm to go over the outline of the proposition. It will at the very lest help to refresh their memory.

In addition, there has been a shift from traditional relationship banking to transactional one-off deals. Businesses can find themselves having in effect to make a fresh pitch every time they need significant funds instead of relying solely on an existing relationship.

Banks must follow strict rules and guidelines when considering financing any venture. After all, banks are all about handling other people's money. For this reason, there are often time delays involved in the decision-making process. That said, banks are in business to do deals, and if your presentation is as clear and concise as possible on what's in it for them, you can help speed up the process and swing the deal in your favour.

All this should inform the way in which you approach a presentation to a financial institution. The larger the sums involved, the more people you will have to influence and persuade. Even if they work for the same financial institution, you cannot rely on them being passed all the information from previous presentations to their colleagues. At best, they may have a summarised version of what you have in mind and of course you cannot rely upon the key facts, as you see them, being presented. Even if they are, it is unlikely that they will have been passed on with your sense of priorities. So, as with all effective presentations, each presentation has to be viewed as individual and tuned precisely to the needs of the new audience.

Raising Initial Capital

Let us look first at the prospect of raising capital for a brand new venture or new project within an existing business. You will of course have a proper plan drawn up, which will indicate how much money you need to raise in terms of initial capital outlay and working capital. The plan should also indicate when you see the business or project breaking even and moving into profit and how the cash will flow during the start-up and transitional phases, right through to profitability. Beware, however, of unrealistic optimism. In my experience, any perceived hype in this area will be seized upon during the question-and-answer session that follows your presentation.

Any financial institution considering backing you will also be interested in the above but will be interested in other issues too, including security for the money advanced, the term over which the money is to be made available and the mix of funding required. Is it all going to be debt? Is it a mixture of debt and equity or is it equity only? Most financial institutions like to see a funding package comprising both debt and equity, sometimes with one organisation taking the debt and another the equity. Whilst in the normal scheme of things, debt can to a certain extent be protected through to taking of security, equity is viewed as more risky. You must expect that a financial institution will be looking to assess and manage these risks. To enable them to do this, they will be particularly looking to you to help them by providing the information they need to make a proper assessment. In this last point lies a criticality when it comes to your initial presentations. Your prospective financial supporters will draw a great deal from the way in which you present when it comes to assessing whether they feel you will report honestly about the bad times as well as the good in future. It is vital therefore to present honestly, accurately and fairly. Integrity is the watchword.

A word now about debt. To the inexperienced person in business, there is a perception that repayment of debt at an early stage is a key desirable in any business plan. When viewed from the perspective of the financial institution, this is not necessarily the case. To a banker, a deal done on debt needs to have a time frame during which interest payments are guaranteed. They need to see a guarantee of the time frame too, no longer and no shorter than the times agreed. Only in this way can they calculate how much profit they will make out of the transaction. An early repayment of debt will upset their profit calculations. If you want to have a provision for early repayment built into the deal, you may find yourself having to pay for it, either up-front or more usually in the form of an extra fee in the event of early repayment. The bank sees this as a way of compensating it for at least some of the extra revenue that would have come in if the repayment schedule had run its full course. After all, the full schedule is what they will have priced the deal on to cover the costs of the initial effort involved in putting the transaction together. It is important therefore in a presentation to understand this key factor. What the bank is looking for is a business plan which is as accurate as possible. Holding out promises of early re-payment paradoxically may not do much to swing the deal. Far better to recognise that financial institutions are in es-sence selling money. Recognise this in your presentation and stipulate over what period both interest and capital are going to be repaid. Demonstrate that you understand the need to stick to the terms of the deal, particularly where interest pay-ments are concerned, and that not only does the business ac-commodate this but also that the business proposition can support such payments.

Putting Your Team Together

You might be forgiven for thinking that, given the technical nature of the information required, all that is needed is to send the business plan off to a bank. This ignores the human factor. In making their risk assessment, bankers and finan-ciers are particularly keen to know more about the principals — the people heading up the business — involved in any lending proposition. In short, they will want to see you and your colleagues and get to know you. This can often present difficulties when putting together a suitable team to present to would-be backers. Let us look at a typical team.

The key member will be the managing director, chief ex-ecutive or executive chairman. She is the conductor of the or-chestra, as it were, and will be responsible for ensuring that the executive directors all pull in the same direction. She

should be able to demonstrate her leadership of these presenters. Note that I say here "leadership" rather than "domi-
nance". Financial backers are always wary of "one man bands"
and those seeking backing have to tread a very fine line to ensure that potential backers do not leave the presentation with
the feeling that they are lending to an individual rather than a
team. Individuals represent vulnerability, whereas financiers
find it much easier to back a well-rounded and obviously re-
silient team.

The next key member of the presentation team is the finance director. In many ways, he has a much trickier role to
play within the team. Whilst he clearly has to be seen as a
team player, he also has to demonstrate a measure of inde-
pendence from the rest of the team. The potential backers are
all looking for reassurance that the finance director has the
integrity and professional standards to ensure that facts
which emerge once the deal is done are accurately reported to
the financial institution.

The institutions expect the financial director to play a key
role in ensuring that bad news is not subsequently relayed
with a gloss which would at best be viewed as wishful thinking, or worse, as downright misleading. The key here is for the
finance director to show that the quality he exudes above all
else is integrity. In the words of one senior banker, "When
things go wrong, we look to the finance director to tell us the
facts, and to tell us early."

Finance directors are often naturally cautious and intro-
spective individuals, and may not be inclined to make waves.
As such, they run the risk of being crushed by the managing
director or chief executive. They also tend to be the weakest
performers in a presentation team, as they are more attitudi-
nally inclined to go into minute detail at the expense of the big
picture. Prospective backers appreciate the potential for the
finance director to be ground down by the rest of the team and

they will be on the lookout for signs of weakness in this department. It is critical, therefore, that the finance director is perceived not only as a fully integrated and properly respected member of the management team, but also that he demonstrates he has the grit required to stand up to his colleagues when it comes to the necessity of reporting inconvenient departures from the original business plan.

Quite often, presentation teams aimed at raising money consist solely of the managing director and finance director. Often the managing director is the key player in developing the project initially. Sometimes this individual can be the inventor or initiator of the particular project. In other words, it will be his or her "baby". A word of caution here. I have met many venture capitalists who have been involved in the backing of new start-ups. The majority of them are very wary of investors with pet projects, citing numerous examples of how their fingers have been burned by putting cash into schemes which have failed to materialise because of the lack of commerciality of the individual initiators. My advice to anyone trying to raise money for a pet project is to take a long hard look at yourself. Are you really too enthusiastic for the project? Would you come across as someone who will not be realistic when it comes to trimming the sales if things get rough? What bankers are looking for is a dispassionate approach. Indeed, some venture capitalists have privately admitted that their experience is less than positive when financing inventors. Some even go so far as to say that when backing a new invention or project in which an individual has invested considerable personal and emotional capital, their first action is to sideline or even remove the inventor or initiator from the field of play. It is a tough world out there, so inventors and initiators may have to curb the excesses of their enthusiasm when making a presentation to raise money.

All this sounds pretty terrible and certainly unfair. However, the plain fact of the matter is that most financiers want to do deals and only make money when they do. If they turn a project down, it is because it is just not right for them and usually that is because the people factors are wrong. Perhaps those promoting start-ups should look to the way in which they put their case across and try to fit in more with the perceived needs of the putative financier. Above all, they should suspend their natural antipathy towards bankers. After all, the acid test comes when you ask the question: "Do I want to be right or do I want to be effective?"

CASE STUDY — MALCOLM CAMERON

A Banker's View of Presentations

In his role as Managing Director of Structured and Specialised Finance at NatWest Bank, Malcolm Cameron is frequently on the receiving end of all manner of professional presentations. He explains what, in his experience, makes a successful presentation and provides some advice on avoiding the communication pitfalls.

"In my position, I see a large number of presentations on a daily basis — from 'beauty parades' when my department is seeking new professional advisers to presentations from management teams seeking financing. Regardless of the exact nature of the request, the presentation has a significant bearing on my decision.

In general, I find presentations invaluable, in order to judge how the company works, what its management style is, and more importantly whether the senior managers have the drive and strategy to justify putting my faith — and the bank's money — in them. The business plans and proposals I see in advance of presentations are all well and good, but seeing this live is my chance to gauge the firm's integrity and expertise.

Often, presentations to City institutions will be carried out as a team. This carries its own particular set of challenges. The structure of each team must be considered carefully. The perfect team should be balanced, not too focused on one area of the business. Each team member must add value to the presentation and play an active role, rather than appearing to have simply come along to make up the numbers. Ideally, every member of the team should be responsible for an area of the presentation, thus giving the audience the chance to view the capability of the team as a whole.

In addition, a presentation speaks volumes about how the group actually performs as a team. For example, I often see pitches where the chairman takes over, displaying an autocratic approach to business. A team leader that doesn't trust his team enough to allow them to speak in public does not instil me with confidence as to the competency of the group as a whole. Also, I know that it is the team members I am likely to have more dealings with in the future, so it is vital I am impressed by their knowledge and ability.

However, stealing the limelight is not the sole preserve of the chairman: I have, on numerous occasions, witnessed one team member overshadowing the others, interrupting them and generally 'showing off'. The members of a team should support each other. Prima donnas, regardless of the fact that they are experts in their field, rarely make a favourable impression.

The team should be well briefed and fully understand the objectives of the undertaking. I remember one occasion when a junior member of the team was charged with changing slides on the projector, but was more interested in staring out of the window than paying attention to the speech, thus forgetting to change the slides when he should. If a member of the company presenting is not interested enough to keep up or doesn't feel it's worth his while, why should I? Equally, disinterest and lack of knowledge can extend to the senior ranks of the team.

I have seen presentations where the senior partner has had little involvement in the project and is there to keep up appearances. This leads to a bored looking partner, who gives the impression that this is beneath him, making me feel it might be beneath me too!

If I were trying to sum up the characteristics of a good presentation, I would say that, in general, those where the presenter has obviously prepared thoroughly and has really considered the message he wants to get across are most likely to be a success. Flexibility of approach is also a good trait — some of the most successful speakers I've seen are those that can gauge the audience's feelings and change the presentation accordingly. By paying attention to the audience's body language and expressions, it may be possible to cut out a part of the presentation on the spot, if you feel you have lost their attention, or expand on an issue you intended to only mention in passing but in which you can see the audience is extremely interested.

Simplicity is also invaluable — conveying a complex message in easily understandable manner is an art form and one which many have yet to master. Keeping things simple is also far more likely to prompt questions than blinding your listeners with science!"

Funding for New Projects

Within established businesses, when trying to raise funds for new projects it is often better to field a three-person team: the managing director, the finance director and a third person who can enthuse about the product or service on an operational basis. This third person, though, will very much have to be kept under control. Whilst the finance director may suffer from the curse of being overly cautious, inevitably the operations or marketing director may be quite the reverse. Much depends on the individual personalities of the presenters. The essential thing is to ensure that each individual recognises his or her strengths and weaknesses and ensures that everyone plays their part in presenting as a team.

From all of the above, one can see that a key element in achieving success in a fundraising presentation is a balanced approach. You will need to be open and you will need to understand what the banks are looking for.

Banks and financial institutions back business so that they themselves may make money. Help them do this by demonstrating in your presentation that you understand the kind of deal they might be looking for. If there is debt involved, the amount of interest paid will vary according to the perceived risk. You should not in your presentation try to understate the risks, but instead should be as open as possible about the factors that could represent a downside to the deal; let the bank themselves make their own calculations. Remember, banks are in a competitive position, so they will want to do a competitive deal where at all possible. However, every contact with prospective backers is part of a process of building trust. It is on the backer's perspective of this trust that the success or failure of the deal will hang. Any attempt to cover up or misrepresent less positive aspects of the business will be found out and even a small lapse can blow mutual trust, no matter how well it has been nurtured. Once such trust is blown, it is very hard to win back. Being open, therefore, is of the essence.

Remember to bear in mind the time frame of deal-making. Experienced deal-makers on both sides say there is almost a tangible rhythm to the way a deal progresses. It starts off with the initial but cautious interest by the potential investor, followed by the trust-building element of the deal while the assertions of the business prospects are assessed and tested. If that all goes well, then cautious commitment comes from the institution. At this stage, the enthusiasm pendulum can swing the other way, with those seeking funds questioning their feelings about the proposed backer. This questioning can be given further force by the presence in the wings of alternative financial support. Finally, there is the eleventh-hour haggling. Just as, in effect, the pen is poised above the paper, comes a hitch hitherto undiscovered by the backer. Sometimes this is just a ploy to swing things more in the direction of the institution, which is hoping that the emotional attachment to the deal on the part of the management will get them to agree to new terms favouring the institution. Finally, the deal is done — signed, sealed and delivered. Everyone breathes a sigh of relief and the champagne corks are popped. At any of the above stages, it is possible for the deal to turn pear-shaped and one of the chief causes of this can be a delay in providing necessary information. Presentationally, this can be problematical. You may, of course, be asked questions at the end of the presentation which you cannot answer. Whilst it is permissible to say you do not have the information there and then, you will however need to supply that information in a timely manner. On the other side of the coin, delay in getting feedback from the financial institution can lead to the management team looking elsewhere.

When making follow-up presentations to different representatives of the same organisation, it is essential of course to ensure that you represent the essentials of the deal in exactly the same way that you did originally. We have witnessed deals fail because potential backers have spotted discrepancies between presentations which they have found hard to reconcile. This can be particularly acute in the area of questions and answers, which is why it is essential to ensure that these too are rehearsed exhaustively as with the presentation itself.

Eventually, if all goes well, your proposal and the shape and structure of the deal which you will have agreed will, once you have accepted it, be taken to the bank's credit committee or some other such senior body for final approval. Ironically, it is here that the presentational tables will be turned. Suddenly the bank officials who gave you a testing time will have to justify the deal to their lords and masters on the credit committee. They know that for them to be effective, they have to be as committed to the prospect as you are and of course the members of the credit committee are hearing the pros and cons of the deal for the first time. If your original presentation has been effective, you will have supplied your bank principals with headlines about the proposal, which they can subsequently use to good effect in their own presentations. Hopefully by this stage the deal-makers will have been persuaded; otherwise they would not contemplate taking your proposition to the credit committee. They will therefore welcome any help you can give them with open arms.

So in essence bankers will have to do their own presentation to persuade the powers that be that your scheme is worth backing. You can help them do this by giving them simple repeatable phrases which sum up exactly what it is you do, why it is worth backing, the overall sums you will need, the debt-equity mix, the rewards and the time frame for the rewards. Be open about arrangement fees and other fees for advisory work by the bank. This is their way of recouping their basic costs at an early stage and demonstrating to their masters at the bank that they have made a return on the deal. This is a necessary cost, which you must build into the business plan. It is a curious position whereby you will essentially be raising money in order to pay it back instantly to the bank, but there it is. That is how it works.

It will do no harm to remind each potential backer that you are talking to a number of finance houses, but do not beat them over the head with this. As interest starts to crystallise, you will have to start making decisions about who you will want to go with. It is tempting to try to play one off against the other, but while this may appear on the face of it to have benefits, such a strategy should be approached with caution. Remember that the world of banking is relatively small and there is every chance they will know the competition.

When completing the presentation, summarise the key points once again and ensure you indicate the time scale for the next steps. Raising money is inevitably time-consuming and diverts managers from the essential task of running the business. It is perfectly reasonable for you to expect the deal to be concluded in the shortest possible time. What is more, good financiers will appreciate and value you as a management team if you demonstrate a clear understanding of the need to complete the deal in a timely manner.

Key Points to Remember

- When presenting to financiers, look at the proposition from their point of view.

- Understand their need to involve others within their organisation and outside if you are seeking large funds which need to be syndicated.

- Be prepared to go over the ground several times.

- Consistency is vital.

- Be realistic when predicting figures, especially profit.

- Give a clear time frame for debt repayments.

- Present as a team rather than a "one-man band".

- Finance directors must demonstrate their integrity.

- Summarise the key points and ensure you indicate the time scale for the next steps.

Chapter 9

PRESENTING TO BANKERS AND FINANCIERS (2): PRESENTING FINANCIAL INFORMATION

In addition to submitting written reports, providing regular figures on business performance, companies are increasingly required from time to time to present periodic financial information to their bankers and financial backers in verbal form. This gives the financiers an opportunity of questioning and testing the figures and the business performance underlying the figures. It often gives the management team a major headache as they wrestle with the challenge of presenting accurately but enthusiastically. As a company grows in size, such presentations become more formalised. Today, public limited companies are required not simply to publish their accounts but in addition feel it necessary to have results presentations, usually at the half-year and full-year points. In some cases, particularly with very large companies, such results are presented quarterly. In these instances, an executive board is never more than three months away from talking formally about their business performance to often quite disparate groups of people who can affect the share price. This can be a tremendous burden unless management teams establish a systematic approach to such presentations.

An issue here which concerns executive directors in large companies is that often quite young and inexperienced individuals working for financial institutions can hold great sway over the interpretation of a company's results. Some less enlightened company directors resent this on the grounds that their share price is subject to the vagaries of what many see as the mere whim of the callow and relatively uninformed. A few directors fall into the trap of letting this resentment show. Clearly, such an approach is not helpful and is downright dangerous if it is allowed to show through in a presentation. It goes without saying that corporate tetchiness has no place in the modern financial presentation. Again, despite the apparent unfairness of the system, you are faced with the simple choice. Do you want to be right or do you want to be effective?

As with all financial presentations, the watchwords are openness and integrity. You have to be honest and tell the truth. However, you may choose to be selective with the truth as long as you do not deliberately mislead your audience. Often, your audience will not want to know the whole truth — that is, every fact and figure — simply because it is not relevant to their needs. They will, however, want to hear facts that are critical to their interpretation of the future performance of the business. This is often a hard judgement call. The majority of directors who have to make regular financial presentations know the value of taking proper time to prepare and talk through the implications of the information they have to present. They also know that it is vital to test the information against their perception of how that information will be interpreted by the audience.

Stock exchange regulations the world over now require that companies are scrupulous in ensuring disclosure of those issues which are pertinent and that could affect the share price. They are also greatly exercised by the principle that one audience should not receive different or extra information over another. All shareholders have to rank *parri passu* when it comes to the information they have disclosed to them. This can present difficulties around results time as, with the best will in the world, it is often difficult to maintain a consistent approach. However, in all material matters, directors must ensure that they plan well in advance what it is they want to say and then stick to the script — even when speaking unscripted. Here then it is vital that there is adequate rehearsal so that individual presenters know their role in the overall scheme of things.

It is worth making a particular point here about the perceived legality of the written word over the spoken word. There was a time when company directors, particularly finance directors, would preface any remarks at a results presentation with advice to the audience that the veracity of the results rested solely in the written document. In other words, the audience should not rely upon any spoken remarks made by the directors during the presentation. The argument for this was sound in as much as the written report will have been pored over scrupulously by the management team and in some cases would have been run past a lawyer and certainly the company's brokers to ensure that the strictures of the regulatory authorities were adhered to. Today it is hard to imagine that such a disclaimer would stand up if there turned out to be a discrepancy between what was written and what was said. Understandably, brokers and analysts do place reliance on the interpretation of the results by the company spokespeople and if you put your foot in it verbally, it would be hard subsequently to insist that your remarks should not have been taken seriously and only the written report should stand testimony to the results. After all, you are using the spoken word to elucidate a set of results in the hope that the business will benefit. If you do not want what you say to be taken seriously, why make the presentation at all?

It is famously reported that, during the Watergate affair, US President Richard Nixon was caught out at a press conference when he apparently contradicted himself over remarks made on an earlier occasion. Nixon mused for the moment, a little nonplussed. Then he recovered his composure and uttered the memorable line, "You know what I said, but I know what I meant!"

Unfortunately for the President, history records that in the long run, such cleverness with words did not save him from his fate.

Sometimes for practical reasons there are separate presenters of the same information for separate audiences. This may occur where, for example, branch offices of a large company have to report to financial institutions in their own region. Often such companies depute a main board director to handle the regional side of the results announcement. As we have discussed previously, it is critical that everyone sings off the same hymn sheet. It would be disastrous, not to say illegal, if, for example, regionally based small shareholders received different information from that given to institutional shareholders. To reduce this likelihood, a useful technique here is to have the company chairman, hopefully taking advantage of his older statesman-like position in the business, mastermind the proceedings. He should take charge of the presentation process several weeks before the results announcement and steer the presentation team in such a way as to ensure that the regional and central presentations do not diverge. Once the broad thrust of the results presentation is known in terms of the results, the salient points to be made in the presentations should be agreed. After that, each team should create a presentation in the light of the expectations of each particular audience. Note here that this procedure, for reasons of consistency, parts company with the normal technique I advise of putting the audience expectations first. Here, the broad thrust of the message comes first and then it is tailored to the respective audiences afterwards.

Once the presentations have been honed and rehearsed, they should be rehearsed once again in front of the other presentation team or teams to ensure that there is no risk of the audiences receiving materially different information on key elements of the results. Usually on hand at this point are the company's PR and financial advisers. Sometimes there can be conflict between these two bodies of advisers. Ultimately, it is down to the company chairman to decide on the correct way forward.

Once the presentations have been settled, it is important that presenters stick to the line that has been agreed so that there are no surprises. The next stage in the preparation process is to brainstorm the kinds of questions that can be expected from each audience. Here it is a good idea to involve the advisers and also have members of other presentation teams ask questions too. When this is done correctly, the questioning is inevitably harder than anything that is received in reality, as those on the inside know exactly where the vulnerabilities are. Only once both the presentation and the answers to the likely questions have been thoroughly rehearsed can the presenters be said to be properly prepared.

When it comes to the presentation itself, the chairman should take charge of proceedings. The presentation should clearly be under his wing and when it comes to the question-and-answer session, he should endeavour to steer questions precisely and with authority. This makes it less likely that the situation will get out of hand, particularly during the question-and-answer phase of the presentation. The chairman's job is to direct questions and buy time for the respondents. They can also, if they are skilled, deal with difficult questions by inviting them to discuss their particular issue offline, outside of the meeting proper.

After a few opening remarks of welcome from the chairman, he should hand to the chief executive who will give an over-

view of the period covered by the particular results being presented. This should not last more than five minutes and it is
probably best to get it down if possible to around three minutes. The chairman should sum up the chief executive's remarks in one or two sentences and hand over to the finance
director, who will then present the figures with simple visual
aids to help people understand the key numbers.

It is important that at every handover, the chairman steps
in to give a short summing-up and lead into the next speaker.
Presentations should not be handled like relay races, with the
speaking baton being handed from one speaker to the next, to
the exclusion of the chairman. Making the chairman the focus
of the presentation adds to his stature and goes a long way to
ensuring discipline and authority over the audience during the
question-and-answer session.

A word here about slides used to support financial presentations. There is a tendency, particularly on behalf of finance
directors who tend to be detail fanatics, to put far too much
information onto a slide. Remember that cognition, the way
the brain interprets what it sees and hears, is much slower
with numbers than it is with words, even amongst those who
are financially qualified. The more numerical information you
put on a screen the longer it takes to interpret. During that
time, audiences necessarily are less focused on what is actually being said by the presenter as the visual tends to dominate the auditory in most people. In other words, if the image
on screen is overcomplicated and requires much interpretation, what is being said by the presenter will for the most part
be ignored.

It goes without saying that the financial information put on
screen should match what is being said in the presentation
itself. Remember the maxim, "do not underestimate the intelligence of the audience but do not overestimate their knowledge". You can be sure that if you do not explain, for example,

extraordinary expenditure, then a sharp-eyed individual in the audience is likely to ask a difficult question. You will have to answer it anyway, so ensure that the information is given in the first place. That way you are better positioned to explain it in terms which have been well thought-out in advance rather than hastily constructed in response to a question.

As a rule of thumb, it is best to keep financial presentations to under an hour. Often, this time can be reduced considerably. The idea here is to keep things succinct. Financial analysts spend much of their time at presentations and they will appreciate brief, to-the-point results presentations rather than wordy ones which are overlong and full of unnecessary information. Typically, a finance director's presentation should run no more than 12 or 13 minutes.

After the short summing-up by the chairman, the chief executive should then take over, thanking the finance director, and launching into seven or eight minutes of her own. Here she can talk about a number of issues around the results themselves, but typical themes can be a particular aspect of the company's operations. Alternatively, she might offer some insight into, for example, the company's acquisitions policy and interpretation of the current market prospects, without of course giving any kind of profits forecast, which would be contrary to stock exchange regulations.

The objective of this section of the presentation is to reassure the audience that the chief executive has all the reins firmly in her hands and knows exactly where she is steering her company. The chief executive should take this opportunity to talk in more depth, say, about how the company views or operates in particular markets. She might alternatively take the opportunity of showing the audience a particular "hero product" that one of her operating divisions is manufacturing or distributing. She can use such products to explain the overall strategy of her group to great effect.

The larger the company, the less likely it is that overall strategies change materially from one set of results to another. By using the above technique of highlighting individual aspects of a company's activities, you can be giving new information to keep analysts interested and foster the notion that you are still a very dynamic company.

All the above is particularly important if you have financial journalists in your audience. Some companies have separate presentations for journalists. This is to be advised if possible, as it does enable you to tailor your presentation more specifically to their needs. Remember, they represent a channel to a number of constituent audiences. These audiences are in effect the stakeholders in your business — your customers, your staff, your shareholders, your suppliers and the larger community. Amongst our clients, we have seen results presentations used to great effect to re-emphasise the company's commitment to quality and service to customers. Others have used the results presentations as a means of settling staff after a period of redundancies. Another client whose shares had been through some turmoil was able to stabilise the share price and show modest gain simply through emphasising shareholder value in their results presentation to journalists. Yet another client used the results presentation to attain wide coverage in the trade press to get the message across to suppliers that they will be rigorously enforcing their suppliers' code of conduct relating to the sourcing of product. And yet a further client company used a results presentation to speak more broadly to a wider community in which its manufacturing facilities were based. Here they were able to give assurances that they were committed in the long term to remaining where they were.

Once the chief executive has finished, it remains only for the chairman to conduct a question-and-answer session. Ideally, this should last no longer than the presentation itself, so if you have a total presentation lasting 25 minutes you should allow up to 25 minutes for questions and answers. The chairman's job is to field these and direct them to individuals. It is a good idea also to have other members of your board present, not necessarily sitting on the platform but in the front row, who can be called upon to answer anything specific that might be raised. It is important, of course, that these potential company spokespeople are properly briefed and rehearsed. I have witnessed many a slick performance by the "top table" marred by an awkward and lacklustre answer from an ill-prepared second tier director to whom an off-the-wall question has been lobbed like a hospital pass. Even if the directors have been properly briefed and rehearsed in likely questions, a good chairman buys time for these individuals by repeating the question, having first indicated who might well be answering. This technique does not buy an awful lot of time, but it can make a real difference to the quality of answer and certainly to the composure of the individual answering the question.

All too often, a chairman on closing a presentation forgets to sum up. He should have prepared in addition to his opening remarks some well-rehearsed closing remarks into which he can interpolate any significant elements arising from the live presentation, particularly points raised during the question-and-answer session. Here the key is brevity. The closing remarks should last for between one and two minutes and contain the salient points once again of the particular results and highlight the particular point of strategy which will have been highlighted by the chief executive. Above all, the audience must be left on a high note, even if the results have not been particularly stunning.

As we have seen, it is possible to achieve much more than simply imparting facts and figures about a company. Even an average set of results, properly presented, can be inspirational and indeed those involved should aim to inspire. There is, however, a difference between inspiration and hype. Hype has no place in any presentation. In a financial presentation it should be guarded against. What the audience is looking for is figures fairly presented but with understandable enthusiasm for the business that underpins those figures. This applies to all the presenters, especially the finance director. You should not rely on the figures speaking for themselves. They seldom do. Similarly, the chief executive should beware of over-egging the pudding and going to the other extreme. Maintain a proper balance. Plan well and rehearse in front of someone who can dispassionately offer a view on how accurately you have achieved the general tenets of a successful financial presentation.

Key Points to Remember

- Expect what you say to be treated with the same credibility as any written information.
- Make sure everyone is "singing off the same hymn sheet".
- Make the chairman the focus of the presentation.
- The chairman's job is to direct questions and buy time for the respondents.
- The question-and-answer session should last no longer than the presentation.
- Keep the overall time to under an hour.
- Prepare separate presentations for journalists.
- Guard against hype.

Chapter 10

THE SEMINAR PRESENTATION

Presenting at seminars is an increasingly popular way of showcasing one's organisation to a broader audience. This certainly is the official reason which companies give for allowing their people to take part in seminars. Another reason is that seminars allow you to see what the competition is up to. One "unofficial" reason for taking part is that, as long as you speak well, it gives you a chance to showcase yourself. This is particularly true in fast-developing industries such as IT and telecoms. Many a new career start has been prompted by a seminar or conference.

Seminars provide an opportunity for people with common interests to come together and exchange ideas in both formal and informal settings. A well-organised seminar or conference ensures that there is a good mix of both types of activity, allowing a number of opportunities for delegates to interact with each other. In this chapter, I will deal primarily with the formal side of the seminar — the giving of the presentations themselves — as these seem to be the ones which give speakers the biggest challenge.

Why Are You There?

Individuals will find themselves presenting at seminars and conferences for one of two distinct reasons. Either they will have chosen to be there themselves or they will have been requested to be there either by the seminar organisers or, as in many cases for new speakers on the seminar and conference circuit, because they have been nominated by their employing companies to speak on behalf of the organisation. In all situations, it is important to recognise that such presentations are essentially selling operations. However, the selling process at seminars and conferences will invariably have to be quite subtle. Indeed, any attempt at a hard sell will usually be frowned upon by the other seminar delegates who will not take kindly to any overt attempt to ram your latest product or service down their throats. However, there are clear opportunities, not only to promote your company, but also to promote yourself, particularly where the seminar consists of participants from the same industry as your own. As I have already mentioned, many successful careers have been built on the ability to present well at seminars and conferences and thus paved the way to promotion or employment in competitive businesses.

For the above reasons, it is worth bearing in mind that just as a good seminar performance can lead on to greater things, a poor performance can conversely be severely career limiting! In short, seminar and conference presentations can yield great benefits but the stakes are high. If you fail to prepare effectively and give a poor performance, it could spell the end of, or at the very least be a blip in an otherwise promising career.

Particularly in modern industries, the ability to communicate across a wide spectrum is often a key determinant of progress within an individual organisation and indeed within the industry itself. It is not surprising then that many first-time seminar speakers approach such events with trepidation. As someone once commented, "Of course I'm not worried about it — it is just my job on the line!" Yet there is no reason why a reasonably competent speaker cannot turn in a really stunning seminar speech. As with all successful presentations, all it takes is a little planning, practice and mastery of some simple but essential techniques.

If you have never made a presentation internally to your own organisation it is, you may feel, unlikely that you will be selected to speak on behalf of your company. Very few bosses will risk an unknown quantity loose at a seminar, no matter how competent they might be at their job. Or so you would think. We have over the years helped a number of quite senior people who had already been through a speaking baptism of fire at a conference and failed dismally. Such an experience is damaging for the company and bruising in the extreme for the individual. Usually we have been able to pick up the pieces but for some people the experience has been so terrifying that speaking again in public is the very last thing on earth they want to do. So the first golden rule of seminar and conference speaking is, *don't do it unless you have already learned your craft and earned your spurs in less demanding environments.* That said, the techniques of successful seminar speaking are simply developments of those employed in other, less demanding forms of presentation and with a little diligence it is possible to excel.

Knowing the Audience

When you are making an internal presentation your audience is usually clearly identifiable. You will often be presenting to a distinct group of peers, subordinates or superiors. With such a well-defined audience, it is a relatively easy task to pitch your presentation in such a way that your audience receives maximum effect. With seminars and conferences it is not quite so straightforward because at such events you will be faced with a number of constituent audiences. All will have to be satisfied if you are to count your presentation a success. Let us consider the likely mix of audiences.

The first audience, clearly, are the delegates themselves. In a way this is the easiest audience to address because you yourself will probably be of that audience. A great advantage here is that unless you are particularly senior and are simply attending the conference or seminar for the duration of your speech, you are likely to be in the position of having to listen to other speakers during the conference. So you in effect are the audience. With this in mind, put yourself in their position. What would they/you want to hear?

In the main, you will surely want to hear new information — that is, facts that you did not already know. Such facts, if properly presented, would add to your knowledge in such a way that you could do your job better or stimulate you to take action to ensure that you did not get left behind.

What you would not want to hear is a litany of tired old platitudes or a rehash of information that is already common knowledge within the industry. You would probably also want to hear a presentation that thoroughly took into account the latest developments in the industry. You would want the speaker to demonstrate clearly that they understood these developments and any remarks were tailored and honed in the light of such developments. This latter point can be very difficult for fast-moving rising industries and we will return to it later on in the chapter.

If you are either quite senior or you represent a firm which is a major player in the industry, the audience is also likely to be interested in your views on the way the industry is going. Your spin on latest developments will be eagerly awaited. Remember that, assuming you are the only speaker from your organisation, for the purposes of the seminar you are your company. Even if you offer caveats about the views you express being personal to you and not necessarily those of the company, beware. Whatever you say and however you couch it, your views will inevitably be taken as the views of the firm.

So you must consider the opinions you express carefully. Another note of caution on the subject of expressing opinion. Although the audience will be interested in your views, you must be able to back up what you say. There is nothing worse than opinion masquerading as fact and audiences, particularly those within an industry, can be very adept at spotting a presentation that is all froth and no substance.

Another issue to bear in mind when considering seminar audiences is the mix of experience, age and status of the delegates. Fortunately there seems to be a trend towards better-defined conferences in terms of who the attendees are. We are now seeing conferences solely for quite narrowly defined audiences, Chief Executives or HR Directors for example. However, many of the more general conferences, even if they claim to be targeted at a particular sector such as HR, can include everyone from training managers to HR Directors in their delegate list. This is understandable, because there is a great temptation on the part of the conference organisers to list as many categories as possible under the heading "Who should attend?" in order to ensure that they get a large enough audience to make the event viable.

Another key constituency in the audience will often be the media. Usually this will consist only of trade press, but there is every likelihood that at certain presentations, and certainly the larger and more prestigious ones, the more general media can be there too. These days, it is amazing the kind of press representatives who turn up, particularly if more general news is having a rather slow time of it. Either way, it is a good idea to have one eye on the media when making your presentation. In this way, your efforts will get a wider audience and, assuming that what you say is of interest and is delivered well, will greatly enhance your reputation to a broader audience. Even in the driest of industries, celebrity status can be conferred on any speaker if their remarks are reported. Curiously, the appearance of your remarks in a printed publication can imbue them with extra resonance and gravitas. Conversely, if you get your presentation wrong and the media report your speech, you run the risk of magnifying the disaster.

Remember too that amongst the delegates may well be potential employers. It goes without saying that their interest in and admiration of your presentation can only serve to increase your "stock" or reputation. Even if you are not planning a move from your current employers, such an improvement in your image in the eyes of potential employers can only be a good thing. Over the years we have dealt with a number of clients who have seen regular appearances on seminar platforms as an essential part of their career-planning strategy — which leads to the importance of another audience sector.

The final segment of the audience will be the conference organisers themselves. These days, conferences are organised on a highly professional basis and there is a real shortage of excellent speakers. Sadly, the majority of conferences and seminars consist of nothing more than a tired dirge comprising uninspiring speaker after uninspiring speaker. If you do well at a particular conference or seminar, there is every likelihood you will be asked to speak again elsewhere and if you are keen to use seminar speaking as a springboard to greater things, an eye on this audience is critical.

Looking at the delegate list is a key element of preparation to ensure that you address the correct constituency. Of course, it is also a good idea to reflect the composition of the audience in your speech, both by talking of the sectors they represent and also maybe picking out one or two individuals who you may know from old — a good way of breaking the ice.

CASE STUDY — LORD MARSHALL

An object lesson on how not to get a presentation right

Conference Board Europe is a well-respected organisation comprised of personnel and human resources directors from large businesses throughout the European Union. Among their many activities are prestigious events to which senior captains of industry are often asked, to give the delegates the benefit of their experience. One such event was held in 1999 at the Café Royal in London. This was a full-blown black-tie dinner in the presence of the American ambassador and at which Lord Marshall, Chairman of British Airways and formerly Sir Colin Marshall, was invited to give the key-note pre-dinner speech.

British Airways and of course Colin Marshall himself are much respected for the way in which they managed to turn around an ailing state-owned industry into what they describe as the world's favourite airline. The audience of Human Resource and Personnel people would be particularly interested, therefore, to hear Lord Marshall's views on the personnel issues involved in developing key people. Hence, the billing for Lord Marshall was most appropriate: "How to retain key people in the millennium." Here was a perfect opportunity for Lord Marshall to share with the audience his experiences at British Airways. As a senior captain of industry he would have been adding to the sum of human knowledge and hopefully providing insights which those present could act upon. Inevitably, senior people in industry also have their own agendas and often use speaking platforms to promote them. Invariably, there is a trade-off between the needs of the sponsoring organisation and the objectives of the speaker. However, on this occasion Lord Marshall got it very wrong indeed. He spent the majority of his speech promoting his two pet subjects, the first being Britain's entry to the euro — the single European currency — the second being why it was important for London to have a Lord Mayor.

> *There were just two sentences relating to the actual billed subject matter of the presentation. Naturally, those present felt he had missed the mark and some felt particularly taken advantage of. Here was a golden opportunity lost and whilst someone as senior as Lord Marshall may well not suffer directly as a result, it did his reputation no good whatsoever. The lesson is, no matter how exalted you might be, you ignore your audience at your peril.*
>
> **Key Lesson**: *Stick to your brief. Even if you have an agenda that you want to push, do it subtly. Don't frustrate your audience's expectations.*

First Contact

As mentioned above, the request to speak at a conference or seminar will come either directly from the organisers or via your employers. Either way, you should use the initial contact to fact-find in order to plan your presentation accurately. As with all presentations, the same key questions apply:

- Who is the audience?

- What do they want to hear?

- What do you want to say?

- Where is the common ground?

This will provide the starting point for your presentation; added to this will be questions to do with how long you are expected to speak for. Most conferences offer 40-minute or one hour slots but in the initial stages this is negotiable. Many speakers often feel they must have more rather than less time. After all, you are the acknowledged expert on the particular subject in hand. It is only reasonable to expect that you should be given what you deem adequate time to convey your knowledge and develop you arguments. This is often a mistake, as in general terms the longer you speak the harder it will be to hold the attention of the audience. Sometimes speakers are offered more time than they feel they can adequately fill. If you really feel you have only half an hour of interesting things to say about the requested subject, there is no shame in admitting that this is the case. Negotiate with the organisers for a speech duration which suits you and your given subject rather than trying to pad it out to an hour or even longer. After all, you are the expert and, when it comes to speaking on any subject, in the eyes of the audience less is usually more. We have often been called upon by an anxious speaker who is struggling to fill an hour slot with material which only merits half an hour. Keep it short and your audience with not only thank you, they will think more highly of you.

Often when the request for speakers goes out, the logistics and running order of the conference are very fluid. The essential point here is to respond rapidly to any request to speak. Not only will the seminar organisers thank you for making their life easier, it will give you the whip hand when it comes to the particular slot you are allocated. Of course, not all seminars are necessarily advantageous for you. No matter how flattered you may feel at being asked to speak in the first place, careful consideration should be given to whether you actually want to take up the invitation. As you get more popular on the speaking circuit, you may wish to pick and choose your engagements. Whatever the case, there are a number of questions you will want to ask yourself before accepting the invitation to speak.

Why you? Are you their first choice or have they been scraping around and have finally dropped on you in the absence of any other takers? If the organisers have asked you for an unusually long speech, might it be possible that they are having difficulty finding enough speakers? In other words, are you there as "filler"?

Do you have the time to devote to preparing the speech required? This is a tough call. We are all busy, so the easiest response (and often that of someone who does not want to put their head above the parapet) is to say no. But perhaps you have to consider this question in the light of the next one.

What is in it for you? What you really have to do is engage in a cost/benefit analysis to assess whether the invitation is really worth devoting your time to. Only you can know the answer to this although your organisation may have a view too. What you should not do is think that, as it is only a small conference with very little potential upside, you can get away with an off-the-cuff performance with very little time devoted to preparation. This way lies disaster because, as we have discussed earlier, you never know who might be watching and it goes without saying that as you are showcasing primarily yourself you will have to give it your best. Better not to make the presentation at all than to do it poorly. Audiences can quickly spot what is known in television as a minimum fee performance!

When would be the best time of day to make your performance? Here, rapid response is essential. If you can get your request in early, you stand a better chance of ensuring that you are not in a graveyard slot. The key graveyard slots are just before lunch and the final speaker of a given day before the plenary session (if there is one at the end of the conference). Another tough slot to fill is the keynote speech at the very beginning of a conference day. Normally, experienced conference organisers recognise that the final slot of the conference can be a graveyard and usually fill it with a panel-based question-and-answer session. Even then, someone has to be the last speaker; better if it is not you facing a tired, jaded and diminished audience.

When asking the question, "What do they want to hear?" the answer will often be conditioned by the time of day the presentation is being made. If you are giving a speech after dinner to a group of people who have been locked in a heavy seminar all day, they probably do not want to hear huge detail about the finer points of your production marketing mix analysis. Something rather lighter would be the order of the day.

Similarly, a presentation at the beginning of a seminar day needs to be lively and relevant to set the tone for the day ahead. From your point of view, it also needs to be remarkable enough to be remembered after your audience has heard another six or eight speakers.

Will you be part of the plenary? Even accepting that many delegates may well leave before the end of the conference, such a question-and-answer session can be a key influencing opportunity and another chance for you to shine in front of your audience. Often space does not allow all speakers to take part in this. Again, if you get your response in early, it may be possible to secure a place on the panel even if the organisers had not thought at that stage of including you.

When is the best time to speak? The majority of people are at their most alert in the morning, so a good slot to try to negotiate for would be the second speaker of the morning or just after the morning coffee break. That way, you will stand the best chance of getting your message across.

Venue, Visual Aids and Technology

It is vital that you get a good grip of the environment in which you are likely to be presenting well in advance of the presentation itself. There is nothing more daunting than turning up to find an auditorium far vaster than you have ever experienced before. Some venues are intrinsically intimidating; large booming halls built decades ago. If all you have been accustomed to previously is presenting in small hotel-room and boardroom environments, then even modern, user-friendly conference halls can appear daunting, if only because of their size. Advance familiarisation with the venue can go some way to overcoming your fear of the large venue. Take time to walk about the hall. Sit in various parts of the auditorium to get a feel for what it is like from the audience's viewpoint. Walk the stage and if possible rehearse what should be the simple act of getting on and off the stage. Many a brilliant performance has been marred by unfamiliarity with exits and entrances.

If possible, have the lighting adjusted to what it will be for the presentation itself. It is amazing how dark it can be backstage, even with working lights. The last thing you want when you are already pumping with adrenaline is to stumble about trying to make your way onto the platform. Watch out for what are these days known as "trip hazards". Bound as we are today with strict health and safety legislation, event organisers are legally obliged to provide a safe environment for all. However, somehow the rules seem always to be different backstage when compared with front-of-house and it is truly amazing how often one has to clamber over obstacles, negotiate trailing wires and cables and squeeze through narrow spaces to find one's way onstage.

It is a good idea also to get a clear idea of the kind of technology that might be available. Most of it is fairly standard, microphones for example, and often you will have little influence over the lighting. Many speakers new to a large conference stage set will be initially fazed by the brightness of the lighting and its consequent effect on their ability to see the audience. Sadly, you will just have to get used to the lighting levels that have been set for the conference. The idea of lighting is to ensure that the audience can see you properly. The fact that it sends you half blind is, I am afraid, of little consequence to those stage-managing the event. Take solace from the fact that you will at least *appear* to be at your brightest and best!

All conference halls and auditoriums are different. Even the most basic equipment such as 35mm slide projectors can vary from simple single-projection operations to complicated, computer-controlled overlap projection systems which produce sophisticated semi-cinematic images. You need to ensure that your visual aids will match what is available. As with all aspects of presentation, planning is vital. The planning process should start well in advance of the due date to ensure that your visual aids are not dwarfed by those of other presenters. Similarly, if you are using computer generation, you will need to let the organisers know the kind of file size you will be using, remembering that it may not be possible to carry all your presentation on one conventional floppy disc. If you use presentation graphics software other than Microsoft PowerPoint, you will have to ensure that their equipment can handle it.

Seminar presenters are often unfamiliar with technological issues, so it is a good idea to nominate somebody in your company to look after liaison of this. This will normally be someone rather more junior than yourself but with more technical ability. When you get the request to speak, it is a good time to think about what you can do over and above standard visual aids such as computer-generated or 35mm slides. Incidentally, overhead projector slides at seminars and conferences are pretty well passé now. If your core presentation has always been done using OHPs, take the opportunity of a major conference invitation to transfer them either to computer or to 35mm slides. The result will be a much more professional presentation than any you could muster using overhead projectors. It will also be a lot easier to deliver, as you will not be bothered with all the business of changing slides yourself. If you are able to nominate someone in your own company to look after the technological side of your presentation, then it is a good idea to ensure that they book the time to go with you to the conference to act as your technical liaison. This will take a great weight off your mind and will enable you to concentrate on your presentation without the worry of the technicalities getting in the way of the performance. I appreciate that this is not always practical, but it is a good objective to set if at all possible.

It is important to think about what other visual aids you are going to use as soon as you get the request to speak. In modern industries, the use of some kind of demonstration can greatly lift a presentation and turn a competent delivery into a truly spectacular one.

Ten minutes is a good unit to build on for a modern presentation. After that, audiences get a bit restless. The secret is to break up the presentation every ten minutes or so with some kind of diversion or gear change. Often, a key part of the success of such demonstrations is to ensure that the business of the demonstrations themselves is carried out by an assistant.

Remember the difficulty of trying to do too many things at once, such as using props? In the same way, when you are making a presentation it is great to have demonstrations, but quite often you put yourself under unnecessary stress if you try to carry them out without having rehearsed them several times until their performance is almost automatic. When you are making a long speech at a major conference, it is courting disaster to try to handle the demonstrations all by yourself. Wherever possible, enlist the help of an assistant who can ensure that all the technicalities run as they should and who can sort out problems if they arise, leaving you to carry on with your presentation, returning to the demonstration if it is appropriate at a later stage.

Of course, rehearsal is essential, as with all types of presentation. Because seminars often take place in an "unfamiliar" environment, some sort of venue rehearsal is called for; at the very least, you should have a technical "stagger-through" with someone from the organisers' technical team. In the business context, we have for several years produced overnight Budget seminars for a leading firm of charted accountants and tax specialists. The seminars are produced just like a television performance and are repeated in a number of venues with colleagues chairing the events. The idea is to provide an interesting interpretation of the British Budget for the accountancy firm's clients, demonstrating the skill and expertise of their specialists and prompting thought and action on the part of their clients in relation to tax planning. We have just 15 hours from when the Chancellor of the Exchequer sits down having delivered his Budget speech to the House of Commons to come up with a one-hour seminar for 8.00 a.m. the following morning. We have to ensure that the seminar will still have resonance and above all offer new insights into the Budget, which the clients will no doubt already have seen on TV or read in the morning paper. It is a tough challenge and it would be very tempting to work away into the small hours trying to winkle out every last twist and turn of the Budget speech and the 70+ press releases which follow. Time, as the lawyers say, is of the essence and there is never enough of it. It is a tough discipline for accountants who are used to being much more contemplative and it would be very tempting to offer more time by cutting down on the rehearsal time. However, all our experience tells us that such a course would be disastrous. We insist on two rehearsals; a stagger-through at about 11 p.m. and a full rehearsal on stage at the various venues at 6.15 a.m. the following morning to be clear before the guests start arriving at 7.45 a.m. We also insist that the presenters get some sleep, preferably getting to bed before 1.00 a.m. So we have to set firm deadlines for when the intricate analysis has to stop and the seminar script has to be put to bed. It all results in a most professional seminar, which has regularly gained plaudits from clients and praise even from other firms who have heard how well the events are received. There is no rocket science to this. It is simply the application of obvious rules in a disciplined manner.

You may well be given the option of using Autocue, particularly at bigger conferences. If so, it is important to look over the points discussed in Chapter 5. The conference organisers and the prompting operator will request a script of your speech a few days in advance of the conference in order that it can be transferred to the prompting software. These days, such scripts can be e-mailed and pasted into the prompting software. This way you can obviate keying errors. However, there are still some systems which are not compatible with standard word processing packages on ordinary computer systems. It is a good idea therefore to run through the script standing over the operator's shoulder (they have their own monitor at their operating unit) to check that the words are transferred correctly. This is also an opportunity for you to adjust the spacing, insert instructions such as [PAUSE] or [SLOW DOWN] or [SMILE]. These run-throughs also ensure that the script does flow as you would want it to when you read it in Autocue mode. Inexperienced users of Autocue often complain that it is not moving fast enough or is moving too fast and it takes time for them to understand and get used to the fact that they are in control. To use prompting effectively takes practice and it is a good idea if possible to rehearse with Autocue off site well in advance rather than use a conference environment as your first exercise in using the system.

Leave Them Wanting More

I have discussed in previous chapters the necessity to ensure that there is a clear "Call to Action" in your presentation and that people are motivated to do something in your favour as a result of what it is you have to say. I have also discussed the necessity to end your presentation with some kind of crescendo. Good speeches are like good music — the listener knows exactly where they are and to a certain extent knows what is coming; there is, if you like, a rising sense of anticipation. They also expect some kind of flourish in the finale. You must take your audience's emotions with you and raise them to a high and leave them feeling that they have dined well but possibly that they could do with a little more by way of wanting to hear you speak again.

If you can achieve this feeling in your audience, you are moving into the realms of oratory and you will be well on your way to becoming a truly effective speaker.

The Wider Audience

Often conference organisers will want your speech in advance in order to distribute it to the delegates. They may also wish to issue your speech in advance to members of the press. They would normally do this with an embargo. An embargo is a device whereby the media undertake not to publish the contents of your speech until after you have spoken. It is normal to place an embargo time identical to the advertised time you are due to finish speaking. Remember, however, that embargoes can be and often are broken, particularly if the news organisation considers that there is real significance in what you have to say and the timing of your speech does not fit in with the deadlines of their particular programme or journal. Politicians and others in the public eye have had to get used to programmes which take themselves seriously and others which are not so serious regularly breaking embargoes. Sometimes they use fig leaf phrases such as, "Later today, Joe Bloggs, chairman of XYZ plc is expected to announce 3,000 redundancies at their Borsetshire plant." If you are concerned about such information leaking out before your speech, then you can employ the following device. In advance copies of your speech, omit the crucial information and insert in capitals,

"CHECK AGAINST DELIVERY". It is a good idea to put a "check against delivery" statement on the front page of the handout in any event, as it allows you to make last-minute adjustments to your speech if necessary. It also encourages the news organisation to send along a reporter, which may offer you a greater chance to influence what is said about your speech, particularly if it is well delivered.

You may also be asked by the organisers for handouts of your slides in order that these too might be reproduced and given to the delegates. Whilst there is nothing wrong with this in principle, it is always best if possible to arrange that these handouts are picked up at the end of your speech rather than before. Otherwise, you run the risk of the impact of your speech being lessened by the audience flicking through to view slides ahead of the time you are actually speaking about them.

I discussed in an earlier chapter how it is important to set aside time before a presentation to calm yourself in order that you give the best to your presentation. Our recommendation is not to mix with the delegates immediately beforehand. However, once the presentation has been given, you will want hopefully to bask in the glory of a successful presentation well delivered. This is also an opportunity to make new contacts who will be keen to meet you now that you are bathed in your new celebrity status as a successful speaker! Make sure you have plenty of business cards with you.

It is a good idea too during the process of analysing the delegate list to try to spy out who you might particularly want to meet immediately after your presentation. The effectiveness of your presentation does not end when you sit down. Take the chance as soon as you can to circulate and buttonhole those who you think can further your cause. The act of speaking up on stage will, for a few minutes at the very least, turn you into a minor celebrity. Make sure you take full advantage of this status, however temporary.

Key Points to Remember

- Prepare early — take advantage of the time between the initial request to speak and the conference or seminar.

- Ensure that you are fully conversant with the various constituent elements of the audience — the delegates, potential employers, the media and the conference organisers.

- Ensure you will not be fazed by the auditorium. Arrange to view it when it is not in use.

- Get to grips with the technology — delegate someone in your organisation to mastermind the liaison.

- Make sure you get the technical crew, including the Autocue operator, on side.

- Ensure advance copies of your speech are "Checked against delivery".

- Try to ensure that handouts are given to the audience at the end of your speech, not before.

- Treat the performance as a piece of music — there should be a clear crescendo at the end and you must leave them wanting more.

- Take advantage of your "celebrity status" after you have spoken and target key influencers.

PART THREE
Internal Presentations

Chapter 11

PRESENTING TO SUPERIORS

When human beings gather, particularly in a business context, their behaviour is very much like that of a baboon colony.
Any one who has witnessed a baboon colony will know that
they can number between 30 and 70 animals and they all
range in size. Baboon colonies are obsessed, it would appear
to the casual observer, with two issues. The first is grooming
and the second copulation. It is the latter which it would appear that, in metaphorical terms at least, human beings also
share in behavioural terms with the baboons.

What happens in a baboon colony is that the larger baboon
always picks on a smaller baboon, forcing it to comply with its
wishes. Very quickly, the smaller baboons get to realise that if
they do not want to be beaten up, they should succumb to the
advances of the larger baboon and they therefore allow themselves to be taken advantage of. They do this no doubt in the
sure knowledge that they can then scuttle off and find a baboon smaller than them.

In the same way during presentations, young baboons, or
indeed human presenters, need to acknowledge the size or in
the case of humans the senior status of the older baboons. It
is, if you like, a form of posturing which many people do naturally but some people forget, particularly if they are young,
bright and intelligent and they are representing a large and
prestigious firm. Sadly, many such modern firms do little to

discourage their young 20- and 30-somethings from the view that they are the masters of the universe and the 40- and 50-something businesspeople who are their clients are inferior and jolly lucky to be getting any sort advice at all!

Successful young presenters remember the baboon colony at all times and knows just how to show deferential but not cringing respect for their elders. This can pay great dividends, particularly during a question-and-answer session, but also if it is applied to the style and tone of the presentation itself. Remember to be humble. There is always a larger baboon out there!

What Do They Really, Really Want?

We have talked in earlier chapters about the relationship between data and information and the fact that most audiences are looking for information, which you will remember is data so sifted, sorted and arranged that they can take action as a result of what they have heard. However, when presenting to superiors there is, in the modern commercial world, an extra something being sought by the audience. Increasingly, they are looking not merely for information but also *insight*. Senior managers recognise that they cannot possibly hope to know all that there is about a given subject. They have experience, which can often play a big part in their judgement. However, they will rely upon you to give them insight into what is actually happening at the coal-face or on the shop floor.

All too often, junior managers feel the need to demonstrate their prowess by going into minute detail. It is the equivalent, in an examination, of showing all your calculations or planning. However, while this is often an advantage in the world of academia, in business senior managers will usually thank you for omitting the detail, preferring instead that you distil out the key essentials of your message. Some senior managers will require the reassurance that you have a grasp of the detail, and it is important to be able to switch into detail mode if so requested. However, initially at least, your spoken presentation should certainly be kept to the basic principles and offer real insightful statements.

From your presentation, the senior manager will inevitably be looking to do his or her job, which is essentially to ensure the correct allocation of limited resources within a company's budget. Most internal presentations are to a greater or lesser extent selling operations. What you are trying to do is give your senior managers confidence that you are doing the correct job and are doing it in a timely and profitable manner. They, of course, have the ultimate sanction of removing your resourcing should they feel either that you are not doing the job well enough or that there are now other aspects of the business that require the funding you have been granted.

I well remember the time when one of our clients called us in to help with internal communications in his business and he summed up our mission as, "Getting my people to tell me in two minutes what it currently takes them twenty to tell me!" Brevity is the key when dealing with senior managers; you must cut to the chase. A key element of the chase is the cash required for any particular project. All too frequently, people shy away from mentioning the cash requirement. We recommend stating up front the kind of funding levels you are looking for or the costs to date of a particular project. This serves to focus instantly the minds of the audience to whom you are presenting. So do not keep them guessing until the end of your presentation. Tell them the costs up front.

A common complaint from those who have to present regularly to their superiors is that the superiors interrupt. This is a difficult one. Certainly, in our work with large organisations, we have gone back to superiors and suggested they give people an opportunity to present effectively without inter-

ruption and be disciplined enough to keep their questions until the end of the presentation. Although our advice is generally taken, there are still exceptions where a senior manager
being presented to by a junior simply cannot contain himself
and interrupts within a few moments of the presentation
starting. This can be further exacerbated if the presentation is
being accompanied by a set of slides which have been printed
out in hard copy and handed to the audience at the start of
the presentation. All too often, a chief executive flicks through
to the end of the slide pack and starts asking questions, thus
totally compromising the integrity of the well-thought-out
presentation. Wherever possible, you as the presenter should
try to request a stay of questioning until the end of your presentation. Whilst this meets with mixed success, it will have a
higher likelihood of success if you explain at the outset how
long your presentation will be. Certainly, if it is no more than
ten minutes, even the most enthusiastic of audience members
should be able to contain themselves. Similarly, as I said earlier, it is not a good idea to hand out a slide pack until the
completion of your presentation.

As with all successful presentations, there has to be a balance between the detail that you give and the overview. Wherever possible you should start off with the big picture.
Commence with a statement along the lines of:

> "This presentation is all about XYZ, which, if imple-
> mented with effect from such-and-such a date, will re-
> quire capital funding of X and should by year two
> provide us with additional sales of Y."

Then you can go through some of the general concepts and
each time drill down into more detail and explanation of how
the concepts work. This is a much better approach than piling
all the detail into your presentation. Keep back the detail for
the question-and-answer session. If you have captured the

imagination of your superiors, they will inevitably want to test your in-depth knowledge of the subject, but let them control the agenda on which they wish to test you. Clearly, this will mean that you will need to be boned up on all aspects of the project. However, this should be a given; otherwise, you would not be in the position of seeking funding in the first place!

Understanding the dynamics of a committee is critical too. In any executive board, for example, there will be stresses and strains between the individual board members. Often, such stresses are taking place beneath an outwardly calm and unified surface, but they are there. The key here is, wherever possible, to address everyone equally. You should not feel the need to kow-tow to any given individual in your audience, save perhaps for the chief executive who is, after all, the ultimate arbiter and can stand between you and your objective. However, it goes without saying that obsequiousness is usually recognised as such and gets you nowhere.

Above all, do not try to second-guess the subtle politics of the audience to whom you are presenting. They are all superiors to you and, although they might on some occasions be at each other's throats, they will psychologically be unified when faced with a subordinate who attempts to play one off against the other. The only loser in such a situation will be you.

Overcoming objections is a core skill of the would-be successful junior presenter. There will inevitably be objections and you should try to think these out in advance. Too many people concentrate on their presentation without thinking through the likely alternative interpretations of the facts that they are presenting. They thus find themselves dumbfounded when faced with objections. Most people find it difficult to think fast enough on their feet to overcome objections, so as much preparation as you can do will definitely help you. The main thing to do is to keep calm, consider the objection, give it credibility, and then offer a cogent response.

All in all, remember when presenting to superiors to keep it simple. Fillet out the key messages but be prepared to go into the detail if required. Remember that superiors are often looking for insight and not just information.

Key Points to Remember

- Leave out the detail; present the essential facts, but be prepared to back up with the detail if requested.

- Mention any cash resources that will be required up front.

- Try to keep questions until the end.

- Don't play politics.

- Offer insight, not just information.

Chapter 12

PRESENTING RESEARCH FINDINGS

A growing reality in the professions and commerce is that the more money involved in a management decision, the more senior managers will want to be better informed before deciding which way to divert valuable resources. Inevitably they will want junior managers to go away and look into a particular issue and then come back and present their findings. Presenting such research can be fraught with a number of problems, many of them to do with the differing audiences you can face when making this kind of presentation.

Academic versus Business Research

Before considering the presentation of business research, let us look first at the traditional case of a pure researcher in a given academic area presenting, for example, a learned paper at an international symposium. The straightforward approach would have been to put forward a presentation which contains the kind of detail your audience of fellow researchers will want to know. Even today, most such presenters still rely on simply reading out dry-as-dust papers in the most boring manner possible. It has almost been a taboo to attempt to imbue such readings with any kind of enthusiasm or excitement. The thinking has always been that such a course would somehow detract from the serious academic status of the paper. However, even in this rarefied area of academic life, that view is

increasingly changing, especially among the younger generation of scientists.

Not so long ago I was particularly heartened when lecturing
a group of young medical researchers from around the world.
They had come together for a conference at an Oxford University college. It was clear that the organisers of the conference
felt they had a desire to improve their presentation skills, even
when it came to highly complex research topics. So we were
called in to run workshops. We and the organisers were im-
mensely encouraged by the response, with the workshops
greatly oversubscribed. The young doctors recognised that,
although they were talking in minute detail about some fairly
complex biochemical processes to a very select audience of
colleagues who were very "into" the subject, there was still a
need to "make it live". They quickly grasped the universal
ground rules that apply to any successful presentation and
transformed their hitherto plodding paper-reading into something rather more exciting. Of course, there was a great deal of
detail and certainly the audience of specialists in the particular field did not feel they were being offered an over-simplified
presentation. There was plenty of depth to each presentation,
but it was all matched to the knowledge and level of understanding of the audience. So, as with all other presentations,
the principal element of adjusting your presentation to the
audience remains the same and this applies whether you are
presenting on medicine or on a business-related topic.

When presenting research, your audience will be particularly interested in elements such as the methodology you employed. They will also probably want quite a lot of detail on the
actual raw data outcomes, statistical variation and other subtle nuances of the research process. For a medical researcher
presenting to fellow medical researchers in the same field,
pitching the presentation is fairly straightforward. You can
make fairly accurate assumptions about the level of knowledge

and understanding of your audience. However, many people doing research, particularly in a commercial environment, can often find themselves presenting to non-technically qualified people or at least to people not qualified in their particular area of expertise.

Here a completely different approach is required, as there may well be vastly varying levels of knowledge, interest and, perhaps most significantly, the basic ability to understand what it is you are trying to convey. This is particularly true when you are presenting findings to, say, an executive management board. Here, the mix of interest and understanding will vary from individual to individual. Typically, for example, a finance director will have a very different set of priorities when compared with, say, a marketing director.

Getting the Order Right

It would perhaps be helpful if we at this stage review the traditional method of conveying research findings using the written word. This method applies equally to learned papers and to business research. The technique has always relied upon an empirical method, using building blocks as it were to construct the overall report. The foundations of the structure will consist of an outline of the background to the research. Why was it considered necessary? Who is sponsoring the research? Were there any presumed outcomes? Does it build on previous research and seek to analyse or re-interpret existing data through updating elements of it? These and a host of other questions need to be answered at the start of your written report.

The researcher might then outline the background methodology used to gather the data. There might be tables showing early results. The next element would be an interpretative layer, with conclusions and recommendations coming at the end. This model is very much how a learned audience might wish to see a paper laid out at a symposium. However, in the commercial world you have to go back to the essential principles of any successful presentation. Above all, you need to recognise that, by and large, the audience's time and therefore attention span is likely to be incredibly constrained.

Another crucial factor is the level of interest of the audience. A common theme running through most businesses that we have helped with their communications is that senior managers as a whole tend to be very bad listeners. This is perhaps understandable. To get to the top, successful executives have to be quick thinkers. They tend to get to the answer to a given problem much more quickly than others do. This is a real challenge to the presenter. Faced with a high-powered senior management team, the presenter simply cannot stop his audience going straight into analytical mode before he has had the chance to get out all the information. This is why presentations to senior management often get interrupted within seconds of them starting. It is all very frustrating for the presenter, who will have spent hours getting the presentation right only to have it disjointed from the very start by constant interruptions. As one client ruefully told us, "To say the top management of his company has the attention span of a gnat is unfair to gnats!"

So, how do you stop this happening? How can you prevent your well-researched findings being ripped to shreds within seconds of you opening your mouth? The first essential factor when it comes to presenting research must be relevance. Senior people can quickly get bored, so it is absolutely useless to put forward research findings that are not relevant to the particular audience. You have to ensure that, from the very start, what you have to say will hold their interest. Indeed, you will have to go further than that. Ideally you will have to intrigue them so that they will want to listen carefully to you and be hanging on your every word.

So when contemplating the presentation of a piece of re-search, ask yourself some tough questions and ensure you come up with robust answers. What is the key headline for this research? What will really grab this specific audience? Which of the particular facts you wish to present are the most relevant to this audience? These are the facts you must put forward first. Wherever possible, they must represent new in-formation or at the very least a new and interesting spin on information already known to your audience. What about the rest of the key results? Can you list them in order of impor-tance? This is the order in which you should present them to your audience.

Winning over a Cautious Management Team

Very early on in the presentation, if you are to hold the atten-tion of your audience you will need to put across some action-oriented facts. This is killer information on which the audience will be able to take a clear action. I say "killer information" be-cause it must be something that hits your audience between the eyes and makes them think; "I never knew that before". This will have the effect of having them listening more keenly to what else you have to say. Remember too that throughout your presentation you must distinguish between information and data. The relationship between information and data is best described thus:

> "Information is data so sifted, sorted and arranged that the listener can take action as a result of what is being conveyed".

Too often people brought up in a research discipline make the mistake of bombarding their audience with vast amounts of data. This is particularly true when it comes to graphics. It is simply no use plucking a table of results or figures from a printed presentation that is designed to be read privately at the convenience of the individual reader and throw it up onto the screen. Remember that graphics should be on screen long enough for the audience to read them out loud twice. This rule is designed for textual graphics. When you are dealing with figures, because the brain has to go though extra cognitive processes, the graphics have to be on screen much longer. If you are going to use complicated tables, make sure you take time to explain them thoroughly. Similarly when it comes to graphs. It is not enough to include the legend or key on screen and expect the audience to work it out for themselves. You will have to explain what each line or bar on the chart means in very simple terms: "The red line stands for our budgeted performance this year and the blue line shows progress to date. The line coloured green is last year's performance." Keep it clear, keep it simple, and above all offer information, not just data. Raw data, remember, is the obsession of the micromaniac and your efforts to shovel vast amounts of data onto the screen and into your presentation will be deeply unappreciated by your audience, who will want simplicity not clutter!

Frequently, and almost by definition, research findings are going to come as a surprise to at least some of the audience to whom you are presenting. Indeed, it would be odd if this was not the case. Also, it is very seldom that research confirms all the prejudices or experiences of everyone. Some people therefore are going to challenge the findings of your research. Whilst this is good for any business, it can often be very unnerving for the junior presenter when faced with a barrage of apparently unsympathetic questions from senior management. In banking, many junior members of management cite an appearance before a Credit Committee with an investment proposal as probably one of the most daunting prospects for a presenter. Often time is short and the committee sits with a cadaverous look and a baleful eye. One presenter described the experience as akin to surveying the fish counter in a supermarket, so unsympathetic are the collective eyes of the committee.

It is the same in other areas of business too, where senior management appears to do its best to unnerve any presenter in the belief that this will somehow crystallise thinking and force out any flannel or waffle. Many clients have told us how unfair they think this is and how it makes them lose confidence. Whilst this is an understandable reaction to what can appear to be very personal criticism, it is unrealistic not to expect some kind of challenging response. After all, what is the role of the senior management in a large organisation? Why are they there and why is it you have to present your findings to them? Why can you not just get on and implement your findings without having to go through the ritual of presentation?

The simple answer is that the role of the senior management is to make choices, and hopefully the right choices, to advance the fortunes of the business over which they have stewardship. They are there to make decisions and set priorities. It is a given that there are never enough resources or cash to do everything a business wants to achieve. Inevitably, someone has to decide which project moves ahead and which has to stand still or which idea has to be rejected or shelved. Often making such decisions can be tough for senior management. They are very well aware of their vulnerability and of the dangers of relying too much on their own experience, which may of course be out of date. To help them come to the right conclusions, they are seeking information and insight from your presentation so that they can make the right choices. They are hoping that, through your research, based on what is actually happening now rather than any historical view senior management might have, they can be helped to arrive at decisions which are right for the business. Serious sums of money are often at stake. They will not, of course, want to make wrong and costly decisions. Is it not then wholly right that they should question closely the results and findings that are brought before them? What would you do if you were in their position?

So, accepting that challenge and questioning are an intrinsic part of presenting research in a business environment is critical if your presentation of research findings is to be a success. That said, when you find yourself being presented *to*, you should remember how it felt when you were on the receiving end, and perhaps resist the temptation to start questioning too early or too aggressively.

Beware of Company Politics

Back to your role as presenter of research. What really matters is how you handle questioning, as this is an essential part of your presentation. It is a good idea to use your own knowledge of the business environment in which you are presenting and your own analytical skills as a researcher to assess in advance which are going to be the controversial elements of your presentation. You may need to involve others in this but be careful about who you choose. There is always a danger that in involving others you run the risk of seeing the gradual leaking out of your research findings before they can be properly presented in totality. Often in such circumstances people get wind of elements of the research findings and if they do not concur with their own particular view of how the business should be run, you may find elements or indeed all of your research being rubbished before it has even been presented. This will not only have a disastrous effect on the particular element of research itself but could well then taint the perception of the entire research project. This clearly would not be good for you as the researcher, but it also would be bad for the company in as much as it will have expended considerable resource on conducting the research only to have it killed before it has been properly presented. Even if your perception that the risk of your research being rubbished is low, it is still good to keep your findings under wraps. If you do not, the impact on your audience will be lessened if they already have some inkling of what it contains. In the human condition, the new always has the ability to create interest. If the contents or recommendations have been telegraphed well in advance there is a risk they will be seen as old hat and not so interesting. So choose your consultative audience carefully. Only present to those whom you can trust to keep your ideas confidential until you have to make the presentation proper.

On occasion, there is also a possibility that, if the person you are consulting with is more senior, they might try to suppress or alter or at least de-emphasise certain aspects of your report. This can be a very delicate area, and you should tread warily if there is any question of altering findings.

It is important that you do not, in a business environment, present research without having due regard for existing processes, customs and practices within the business. You need to be able to reflect and almost celebrate the surprise with which some people will receive your research in order to help those individuals keep an open mind regarding any action that might be taken as a result of your findings. What we are really talking about here is the management of change and of expectations. It is the human condition that we tend to believe that things will continue as they always have. Most people find any change difficult and challenging and are innately conservative. Change involves risk. It also means delving into the unknown. Most people fear the unknown. Even in companies, which proudly boast, "In our firm the only constant is change", there will be many who find the process of change challenging, particularly if it directly affects them. You have to have due regard for this when presenting the more controversial elements of your research.

In short, you have to go gently with your audience when asking them to overturn time-honoured beliefs and traditional ways of thinking about business issues. Acknowledge the potential difficulties by using softening phrases such as, "I appreciate that this is a break with what we've been used to", or, "I was surprised by this particular outcome too until I looked into it more closely", or "Clearly this may initially be hard to implement", or "Getting our people to buy in to these findings will be challenging". The essential point here is not to underplay the research findings themselves. These you must stand by. What is important is to be sensitive to the impact such findings might have on the organisation.

Implementation Costs

Another area where research can founder, and risk rejection of its recommendations, is that of cost. One of the easiest ways of killing off unpalatable research findings is to suggest that, whilst they may have a grain of truth, the recommendations indicated by such findings would be totally uncommercial and thus impractical. It would be useful, therefore, in your presentation, to nod in the direction of the commerciality of any particular findings.

Presenters often try to soften the blow by using phrases such as:

> "Clearly the implications of this element of the research are such that we would need to find significant funds and shift resources from other parts of the business in order to carry through the necessary requirements for change. However, it is important to examine and assess the long-term risks to the business if we do not make changes."

Whilst the sentiment behind such a statement is laudable, it is much better to be more direct:

"The research shows we have to make some tough choices when it comes to shifting our spend. But if we do not act there is a real risk we could live to regret it."

By using some such softening phrase, you are leaving your audience with the thought that it will still be their decision in terms of the actions taken and that they are still in control, as it were, of the action taken as a result of the research. This is a critical issue if your research is not to be sidelined.

Another good technique to ensure "buy in" by the audience is to solicit their feedback at points of controversy using phrases such as "I and/or the research team would be most interested in your views on this particular element and its implications." As you will see, what I am suggesting is that to be successful, a presentation of research results has to make the leap from the research team to the wider commercial operation by involving people in the interpretation and the analysis of the results. Whilst properly conducted research is always by definition accurate, the commercial elements, in terms of what action can be taken, are open to wide interpretation. What is critical is that you do not lose the outcome of the entire research because of under-involvement from your non-research colleagues in a commercial environment. Soliciting feedback at an early stage is vital. Remember the baboon colony principle outlined in Chapter 11?

Quite often, you may need well over an hour to present a major piece of research. If so, remember to break it up into bite-size pieces. A good way to do this is to plan in a pause for questions and feedback every ten to fifteen minutes or so. This is all about the psychology of the new. Whilst new things tend to excite people, they also frighten people. As I have already identified, most people are intrinsically opposed to change. By definition, good research implies the need for change in an organisation. If you plough through an hour-long presentation without any pauses for feedback, you will inevitably run the risk of alienating your audience. This will be particularly the case if you find yourself presenting killer facts at an early stage, which will understandably prompt a response from the audience. You must allow them to vent that response at an early stage rather than bottle it up as you plough on through the rest of your presentation.

Each start of a new segment of the presentation represents a new beginning for your audience. Hopefully, if you stick to the rules for grabbing their attention, you will be able to reinvigorate their interest in your presentation. In this way, even the most complex of research can be made accessible for the widest possible audiences.

Remember that, as with all successful presentations, when presenting research you will want your audience to take action as a result of what you have told them. The challenge is to make sure the action is what you want to happen. If you have planned your presentation correctly, the last person to be surprised by the outcome will be you, because you will know exactly what to expect.

Key Points to Remember

- Make sure your presentation is relevant.

- Pick out the key headlines to the research.

- Don't load your presentation with piles of meaningless data

- Take soundings in advance of potentially difficult areas.

- Confront potentially controversial issues early on.

- Offer insight and not just information.

- Pause for feedback every ten to fifteen minutes.

- Be prepared to be challenged on some of your findings.

- Don't run the risk of losing your presentation impact through leaking early results.

- Your findings will probably imply some element of organisational change, to which people are often averse. Be sensitive to this.

- Ensure you address the commercial implications of your findings.

- Don't present in such a way as the audience is disenfranchised from the decision-making process. Leave it open to them to take action decisions.

- Make use of "killer information" which will spur the audience on to take action.

- Try to ensure that you approve of the action taken.

Chapter 13

PRESENTING AT AGMS

Facing shareholders at AGMs constitutes an important part of every board director's working life. But it is an activity few approach with relish. If you know you will be required to speak at an imminent AGM or results presentation, it can be a daunting prospect. AGMs offer the prospect of facing shareholders eyeball to eyeball. Often the shareholders, particularly those with small holdings of stock who have no other opportunity of talking back to the directors, see this as their one chance in a year of getting their own back.

Little wonder then that an approaching AGM can all too often instil a sense of dread in even the most experienced director. This anxiety is, of course, quite understandable. Any type of disruption or mishandling of questions is likely to be reported in the media with glee. Moreover, AGMs provide the opportunity for shareholder activism, with small pressure groups often attending with a specific agenda of issues they intend to raise. Reports of badly handled situations of this nature abound — for example, the case of the chairman who declared the meeting closed after a particularly demanding round of questions. The resulting sit-in protest and police intervention led to uncomplimentary coverage, not only of the day's events, but also of the underlying issues worrying shareholders. Such occurrences, along with the generally high-profile nature of the AGM, add to the sense of apprehension surrounding this event. So how can companies ensure their top executives are prepared to deal with the rigours of communicating with the financial community, be it once a year at the AGM or at more specialist briefing sessions? A number of general rules can help make the whole experience less painful for all involved.

One of the first things to remember is that, as a community, the City of London and indeed all other financial communities hate surprises. The responsibility of the public company is to be prepared to adopt an honest stance, particularly with its major shareholders and the analysts. It is very rare that companies get away with being less than truthful with their shareholders, and once lost, confidence is notoriously hard to regain. To this end, you must ensure that presentations are candid and forthright, and while competition or security reasons may prevent you disclosing everything, avoid misleading at all costs.

This honesty must extend to the sharing of bad news with shareholders. Often the problem itself is less of an issue than the way the organisation is seen to be dealing with it. Being frank about problems enables senior management to display the strategy by which it means to handle them, which is far more likely to gain the financial community's trust than keeping quiet and allowing a full-blown crisis to develop.

However, even when the message is negative, ensure that the way the subject is broached is just the opposite. As executive chairman of Admiral plc, Clay Brendish, says: "The importance of a positive approach must be impressed upon us all — it is vital to remember that we are senior representatives of a good company and ambassadors for it."

Remain realistic at all times. By all means divulge future plans and strategies for dealing with current challenges, but be wary of raising expectations above what the company can viably achieve. Moreover, shareholders buy the future of a company, so while presentations should be forward-looking, they should also be solidly grounded in fact. Raising expectations can turn good results into poor ones simply because investors were expecting greater things.

In addition, think carefully about content. Being a great orator is all very well, but on these occasions audiences want to hear something of substance. Take time to think about the main messages to be conveyed. It is essential to run through any presentations with colleagues to ensure key messages are effectively communicated.

I discussed in earlier chapters how dealing with questions in a positive and welcoming manner is vital if you are to leave a lasting good impression. Apart from the message that companies want to communicate at AGMs and other business briefings, they also need to give due consideration to the interests of the audience and the questions they are likely to be asked. Before the event, it is important to take time to think of all the possible questions that may be asked. Look back over the past year's events and check any press exposure to remind yourself of any areas that may come under shareholder scrutiny. Few companies can claim to have no tricky subjects on which they would like to avoid questions. These "hot topics" come in many guises — for example, a fall in profits, rumoured redundancies, or talk of violations of human rights or environmental laws.

AGMs provide an ideal opportunity for disgruntled shareholders to voice their discontent and demand reassurance on issues that have been troubling them. Directors must therefore be able to handle sometimes difficult situations, dealing effectively with any hostile questioners while conveying the company's core messages. Below are a few of the more common questions that may be asked and standard lines companies can take to provide a satisfactory answer. Obviously, this list is not comprehensive, nor should the answers necessarily be followed to the letter, but rather adapted according to particular circumstances. Organisations and situations differ, and companies should try to include as much company-specific information as possible when answering.

"How can you justify the vast salaries and bonuses board members are receiving?"

"We have to pay the market rate for the job. It is vital to our shareholders that we attract and retain the very best people, both in good times and in bad. The remuneration committee, chaired by an independent non-executive director, ensures that we get the pay rates for our executive team right — not too much, not too little. Bonus structures are set so as to align the interests of the management team with those of the shareholders. Your management team must be incentivised to deliver the best returns to you as shareholders."

"Profits have fallen this year. What are you going to do about the company's trading position?"

"Our executive team is constantly striving to maintain and improve the profitability of the company. We are examining all our operations and everything is up for review — nothing is sacrosanct. We go to great lengths to find out possible ways to improve the running of the company and deliver increased profits. Our management team is focused on this goal for the coming year. Naturally, we are affected by the trading climate in the markets in which we operate. But our policy is aimed at creating steady and sustained growth in good times and bad."

"Is it true that you are planning to make some redundancies and, if so, why?"

"A well-run company always aims to have a workforce appropriate to its needs. That means having the right numbers of people with the right mix of skills. Inevitably, staff numbers will vary. Redundancies are only ever made after very careful consideration, and

only once we have explored all the alternatives. Having said this, we have no current plans for redundancies."

"Is it true that you might soon be subject to a hostile takeover bid?"

"I take it you are referring to rumours that have appeared in the press. Inevitably, this amounts to nothing more than speculation, and we do not comment on speculation. However, I will say that the company is not for sale."

"Why do you pay such huge severance pay to executives who are clearly being pushed out because of poor performance?"

"Where payments are made, they are in accordance with the contractual agreements already in place with individual employees. We seek the best possible severance terms for the company, but we do not discuss individual arrangements for obvious reasons."

"How can you defend the company against recent accusations of unethical practice?"

"The company will never knowingly support unethical conduct. We have a code of conduct that is well known to all our stakeholders. If we find our code is being broken, we will take appropriate action."

Remember that AGMs are often regarded as "open season" on the directors. So you may get hecklers. Provided your team is fully prepared, there should be little chance of you being thrown by any particular question. If you are faced with a particularly tricky question, however, these are the best ways to deal with it:

- Take time — although not too long — to think of an appropriate response. If you cannot answer the question, explain that you do not have the information to hand, but offer to find out the answer and respond promptly after the presentation.

- If you do not want to answer the question, do not ignore it or skirt around the issue, but explain politely that you don't intend to answer. You may choose to add a softening phrase to keep the audience on your side, such as: "I fully understand why it is that you're interested in this, but I'm sure you can appreciate how useful that information would also be to our competitors."

- If someone challenges you, answer the question, but don't allow a dialogue to develop. Try not to be rude, aiming instead to "kill with politeness". Respond briefly to the point raised, then, politely, make it clear that the discussion is closed by physically turning to another part of the audience and carrying on without a break.

Assuming a company is properly prepared, AGMs can be handled effectively, whatever the fortunes of the organisation at that time. The most important point to remember is that AGMs are a unique opportunity for companies to publicise their good work and reassure shareholders and other interested parties of the health of the organisation. As such, they should always be viewed in a positive light. As with any occasion, its success falls mainly into the hands of the host.

CASE STUDY — XYZ PLC

How to get an AGM wrong

What is the point of Annual General Meetings? None whatsoever, if all the board is going to do is sit on the platform like stuffed dummies. That was the verdict of one disgruntled and crusty shareholder at the 1999 XYZ plc Annual General Meeting.

It had all started off quite boringly in the gold and crimson splendour of a livery hall in the City of London. The chairman rose under a splendid glass chandelier to address an audience of fewer than 50 shareholders, which contained more than its fair share of what are known in business as the tea and biscuits brigade — those who turn up as much for the hospitality as any particular interest in the governance of the company.

The chairman didn't exactly cover himself in glory, reading from a very precisely worded script, which had clearly been written for him by his brokers. There was little or no eye contact with the audience either from the chairman or from members of the board. If anything, they looked thoroughly shifty. One of them held his head in his hands for much of the chairman's remarks. Surely no real demonstration of much support for their esteemed chairman, who has built the business from his founding shareholding to something which has created a personal wealth to him of in excess of £50 million. Another director sat with his eyes downcast throughout.

But not to worry. The chairman had a languid and laconic style; he managed to speak almost without moving his lips. He and, indeed, his fellow members of the board gave the impression of not being so much a board as thoroughly bored.

They almost got away with it until the chairman asked for questions. There were none, except from one shareholder, who had not been given his yellow voting card. So on they went, but they were not to reckon with one thoroughly disgruntled shareholder who, when it came to the re-election of directors, asked very pointedly and in an extremely loud voice, "Why was it the board all sat there like 'stuffed dummies'?" Granted, they had been introduced but none of them moved a muscle when their names were called out. How were the audience of assembled shareholders to know who their directors were? "They should stand up," said the shareholder.

Rather sheepishly, the first director up for re-election stood up, adding in a somewhat testy way, "I can assure you, sir, I am not a dummy." One by one, the two other directors up for re-election were forced to draw themselves up to their full height and acknowledge the presence of their esteemed shareholders.

It was all a bit of a laugh really, but it added up to 15 uncomfortable minutes, more uncomfortable than most Annual General Meetings.

Key Lesson*: Take all audiences seriously. Ensure that you rehearse your team in how to look attentive and interested in both the speakers and the audience.*

Key Points to Remember

- As your company's representative at an AGM, it is important to take an honest stance with the shareholders.

- Don't create unreal expectations. Everything must be grounded in fact.

- Rehearse with colleagues beforehand.

- Be prepared to answer difficult questions on controversial issues.

- If you don't have the answer to a question, ensure the questioner that you will find out as soon as possible after the presentation.

- Remember that AGMs can create positive publicity and enhance your company's reputation if they are handled well.

Chapter 14

INSPIRATIONAL PRESENTATIONS

As people climb the career ladder and become increasingly senior, inevitably they become responsible for more and more people. This is happening to individuals at a younger and younger age. It is not unusual, for example, for someone in their 20s to have 60, 100, or even 500 people in a division for which they are responsible. They cannot know them all very well and anyway in a well-run organisation there should be only half a dozen direct reports to the overall boss. However, quite rightly, people in such positions do feel the need to connect with the individuals whom they are leading on a regular basis. Thus, forward-thinking organisations encourage regular sessions whereby the top managers can communicate in a formal and informal setting with their people. Inevitably, the larger the number of individuals reporting, the more didactic, or one-way, the presentation runs the risk of becoming. Notwithstanding this, such presentations can be hugely motivational and can make a real difference in terms of squeezing extra percentages of performance out of an organisation.

So what are the key elements of an inspirational presentation? Firstly, whilst the boss may wish to convey his or her view of the world, it is important for them to remember to motivate rather than hector. Too often, we have seen individuals who, probably because they are highly driven themselves, leave audiences with a feeling of inferiority. This is because the speaker, in stressing how brilliant and clever he or she is, only serves to highlight in the minds of the audience how inadequate they are. A truly inspirational leader will be adept at celebrating the team's abilities rather than hold up his or her own achievements in the hope that they as lesser mortals might struggle and strive to achieve similar greatness. The only way to inspire people is to empower them to strive for even greater heights. This can only be done through encouragement.

Of course, many still argue that all inspiration falls back sooner or later on the old technique of "stick and carrot". Clearly, and I have had this discussion with a number of leading managers in business, there needs to be a balance between the two, and the debate will continue for ever about how much stick there should be as opposed to how much carrot. Some would argue that the ratio of stick to carrot should vary according to the employment market. When there is high unemployment, the argument says you can add more stick and less carrot. When employees can take their pick of jobs, then more carrot has to be built into the equation. In reality, this is too simplistic an argument. In very few industries these days is labour a raw material to be set on and laid off as a business adjusts to the vagaries of the marketplace. Today, particularly in professional and white-collar businesses, a workforce represents a significant investment on the part of the employing company. For a start, they will have had considerable training. They will represent the collective knowledge of the business. It will be hard for an employer to see that wasted. Hence the need to inspire through encouragement and empowerment.

Despite this, sadly, I have witnessed far too many examples of so-called inspirational speeches consisting almost entirely of stick and very little carrot! These presentations are also usually one-sided in terms of the openness the presenter shows to any ideas put forward by the audience. I have often witnessed a hectoring speech followed by a request for questions that comes out more as a challenge rather than a genuine manifestation of the speaker's willingness to expand further on their subject. It beggars belief how some senior people in management close down questions even though they have gone through the motions of inviting the audience to make points or seek elaboration on a particular issue raised. It seems such speakers prefer instead to follow the edict of, "When I want their opinion, I'll give it to them."

Many presenters in senior positions fall into this trap without even realising it. There is no doubt that many questions raised by a junior audience will appear callow and naïve to the experienced individual, but at least such questioning shows that the audience is thinking about the subject.

So if you are in a position of having to make a motivational presentation, you must ask yourself key questions about your attitude towards your audience and, of course, give yourself honest answers. A major issue here is that you must respect your audience, no matter how junior they are. In talking to junior managers about the qualities they admire in a speaker, a recurring theme is that the speaker treats the individuals with respect. It is a rare quality, because it is so easy for confident speakers in a position of seniority to forget how insecure the more junior members of their audience may feel.

A good inspirational presentation starts off by celebrating success rather than dwelling on failure. This is sometimes difficult to conceive as a principle, in as much as often the requirement for a motivational presentation arises because of something that has gone wrong or something which could be done better in a business. There are, however, very few situations, no matter how badly things have gone wrong, where it would not be possible to find something to celebrate in terms of what has been done correctly. This is your starting point. It will pleasantly surprise the audience who, not being stupid, will realise that things are not all as well as they should be.

That is not to say that you should offer a Panglossian view of the world in the face of clear disaster. However, it is all about being cheerful in the face of adversity. After all, when it comes to being upbeat or downbeat, it is on how you sound and on your general demeanour that your audience will take its cue. Remember how former UK Prime Minister Margaret Thatcher started her valedictory speech to a packed House of Commons after losing the Tory leadership? As MPs waited uncomfortably for what they imagined might be a corporate handbagging from the newly deposed Prime Minister, Mrs Thatcher turned the tables on them by breaking the ice. "It's a funny old world . . ." is how she started off. It brought the house down and relieved the obvious tension in the Commons although there were probably more than a few Conservative MPs who were forced to look again very seriously at any part they might have had in her downfall.

CASE STUDY — J.F. KENNEDY

Empathise with your audience

In 1962, John Fitzgerald Kennedy, one of the youngest presidents the US has ever seen and the darling of the Western world, stood on the Brandenburg gate to address the people of Berlin. He, of course, appeared as the most powerful man in the world and leader of the country which was largely responsible for the downfall of Germany during the Second World War. This fact was well within the living memory of most of those present.

How did he approach his speech? Well, he immediately celebrated the courage and bravery of Berliners through, for example, the Berlin airlift and beyond. He used these words:

> *"All free men are citizens of Berlin. Therefore, I take great pride in saying 'Ich bin ein Berliner'."*
>
> *Students of German will know that the President's speech writer rather let him down on the day, as evidenced by a German general standing on the platform next to the President, who collapsed with laughter as he heard this. What the President should have said was, "Ich bin Berliner" — the correct German phrasing to indicate you come from the city of Berlin. By saying "Ich bin ein Berliner", the President was of course saying, "I am a doughnut"!*
>
> *Despite this gaff, the audience and even the German general acknowledged that the US President had made a real attempt to empathise with his audience and also celebrate their language. So they nodded approval of his speech and cheered him enthusiastically.*
>
> **Key Lesson**: *Wherever possible, celebrate the greatness of your audience. It pays great dividends, even if you do not get it precisely right. After all, it is the thought that counts.*

Having got your audience on side by celebrating how well they have done despite a difficult situation, you can then move on to how you believe it will be good for them to change behaviour in a certain manner. Again, this must not be done in a hectoring manner; rather, it should be a demonstration to them of your belief that they have the ability to deliver at a much higher level and in such a way that will not only benefit the organisation but them as individuals. What is called for here is an element of leadership. A good leader is someone who, even when addressing large groups of people, talks to them as individuals so that when they leave the presentation they each feel a one-to-one bond with the leader.

Leadership is clearly an important prerequisite for inspiration. Again it is important that you demonstrate this through confronting issues which you will know through advance analysis to be uppermost in your audience's minds.

CASE STUDY — LORD MOUNTBATTEN

Leadership as morale-booster

During the Second World War, this was particularly well illustrated by Lord Louis Mountbatten. There was great concern about the morale of the British Army in Burma, which tended to be overlooked by the powers that be back in Britain, who had their focus rather more on the European theatre of war and the Eighth Army at El Alamein. The army in Burma referred to themselves as "The Forgotten Army". Such was the concern about their feelings that Lord Mountbatten was asked to go on a morale-raising tour of the army's various positions in south-east Asia. A lesser man would have gone from camp to camp simply telling everyone what a good job they were doing, no doubt telling them to "Carry on and keep a stiff upper lip". Lord Mountbatten was made of sterner stuff and understood well the need to confront the issue uppermost in his audience's minds. So in every one of his talks to the troops, he started off by saying, "I know you people believe you're the forgotten army. I'm here to tell you that you are not . . . because nobody has ever bloody heard of you!" The result of this was instant laughter and knowing nods from his audience who recognised that here at last was someone who understood their feelings. From that point, Lord Mountbatten had them eating out of his hand and morale was quickly restored.

*   **Key Lesson:** *Confront the issue that is uppermost in the minds of the audience, especially if it is controversial and challenging.*

Another key element of motivational or inspirational presentation is the sharing with the audience of facts to which they are not normally privy. The secret here is to steer them to the conclusions you wish them to make but fall short of actually making those judgements for the audience. The idea is instead to leave them as individuals to make the judgement for themselves. Beware, however, when imparting privileged information that you are not so selective that you stand accused of misleading your audience through giving them only partial facts. Here, as with all things, honesty is the best policy. However, subordinates will understand that there are some areas where it is difficult for you to provide all the information.

I have already mentioned the challenge when addressing large audiences in not making the presentation didactic and one-sided. Inevitably, you will want to open yourself up to questions and answers. As I have already discussed, this is often problematic for strong managers. They feel the need, even in these sessions, to assert themselves. The secret here is to change from speaking mode into true listening mode. Good managers know that to be really effective there has to be genuine two-way communications during such sessions. Your audience has to feel involved and valued, especially if they have taken the trouble to ask a question. If standing up and presenting to a large audience is challenging, asking a question — and certainly being the first to ask a question — can be even more daunting.

It is important, therefore, that questions are sought in an open and encouraging manner. Many strong presenters in a superior position crush potential questioners through apparent aggression, to such an extent that the audience sits in stony silence. Some cynical managers can of course see this as an advantage in as much as the silence can be interpreted as acquiescence. Simple analysis tells us this is clearly not the case. All that has happened is that the audience has bottled up their frustration.

Remember, the questioners, by definition, will be seeking information about a subject which they know less about than the presenter. To ask a question against such a background requires courage. All questions should be treated with courtesy, no matter how apparently ridiculous they may seem.

There will, of course, be those in the audience who will seek to ask questions only to aggrandise their own position. As the presenter, and indeed as the senior manager, you may feel tempted to put this particular type of questioner down. Do not. Treat them with equal courtesy. You can usually rely on the audience to sort out those who ask self-serving questions simply because they like the sound of their own voices. If you try to sort them out, you may find the audience turns against you. By demonstrating courtesy, even to the most annoying of questioners, you will do far more for your own status.

A common mistake made by presenters is to believe that the presentation is over once the questions and answers have been dealt with. There is one final *coup de grâce* which needs to be delivered. When you have dealt with questions and answers, ensure that you have pre-prepared a final summing-up. Ideally, this should last for around two minutes and should encapsulate the main points, stressing the motivational and celebratory. Such final summings-up can have tremendous impact on the way you leave your audience. You can send them away on a high note, fired up and hopefully ready to move forward to greater levels of performance.

Video Presentations

With large organisations, particularly where there are operations across a number of locations, a senior manager might choose to make a presentation by video or on occasion by satellite link. Clearly there are advantages to this. Firstly, it is a cost-effective use of the manager's time. One video or satellite link can travel the world. Additionally, such links offer the prospect of ensuring each member of the audience receives an identical message. Such messages can also be organised so that they are disseminated simultaneously. This can be important if, for example, the company is going through a major structural change such as a merger or take-over. The same information can where appropriate be released simultaneously to the media to ensure congruence between the internal and external messages.

The disadvantage of a video or satellite link presentation is that they can be perceived as impersonal. While some chief executives positively relish the prospect of being beamed into a staff conference on the big screen, this can backfire if the audience feels they are being short-changed. They are more likely to be understanding if it is clear that geography makes it difficult for the speaker to be presenting the auditorium. For example, workers in a UK business will probably accept that a video or satellite link is a reasonable price to pay for hearing more frequently from a chief executive who is based in the US.

If you are being videoed or live-linked, the key issue to bear in mind is that you are, to all intents and purposes, appearing on television. Television is a much more intimate medium than standing up in a large conference hall and delivering a presentation, so you will have to adjust your speaking style to make it more cosy. Former US President Ronald Reagan was a past master at this. He used all his acting experience to deliver "state of the nation" fireside chats to his "fellow Americans", using the medium of television to devastating effect.

The lesson here is that in essence you will have to approach your presentation much more gently, in keeping with talking on a one-to-one basis with someone. One piece of time-honoured advice is that you must have a "love affair with the camera". This is perhaps a little florid, but the sentiment is not too wide of the mark. You have to imagine that the camera is a real person and you must try to influence that person.

So in essence you will have to soften your voice; this is not the medium for a loud, highly projected approach. Talk gently to the camera and try to be persuasive. All the usual rules apply about keeping the message simple and ensuring that you do not overburden the listener with too much detail.

Talking effectively to camera is a real skill; you will need a lot of practice and several rehearsals to get it right. Wherever possible, employ the services of an external video crew with a good director. Only they will have the courage to tell you when you have got it less than perfect. After all, it is a very tough call for most people to offer their boss effective and constructive criticism on television technique. It is even tougher for most bosses to take such criticism, although they are more likely to if it is coming from a seasoned professional. There have been many occasions when I and my colleagues have been called in by Directors of Corporate Affairs to deliver helpful but unpalatable style messages to proud CEOs!

A few years ago, an Irish government minister and presidential candidate was implicated in a political scandal. He responded by going on the national news; at one point, he turned directly to camera to plead with the audience, denying the allegations. The effect was totally counter-productive, and even fewer people believed him. He subsequently lost the election.

In short, treat the opportunity to present on video with great care. It should only be used in certain circumstances. Only seasoned speakers should attempt it and then they should be prepared to moderate their style to fit the intimacy of the medium.

How to Become a Celebrity Speaker

Over the years many people have asked me how to become a celebrity speaker. Much of this book has been about elevating your presentation skills to that of oratory and in time you will find yourself in increasing demand as a speaker. So what are the requirements for a celebrity speaker or speaking guru? Well the first thing is that you have to be a confident speaker, and particularly an entertaining one. Speakers are initially asked to speak for a number of reasons. The first reason is usually their status, which is conferred on them by the position they hold within their business. Once you have been seen by a few audiences and have been successful in "wowing" them, demand for your services will start to build. Celebrity speakers transcend the normal rules of presentation by becoming so successful at entertaining their audiences that they become a name in their own right.

It is within the gift of everyone to be able to do this, should you wish to do so. However, many senior people in business take the view that they simply do not have the time to go on "the celebrity speaker circuit". I suspect, however, that many of them are just too frightened to go for it. The trick here is to use your status to your own ends. Indeed, I have had many clients who have gone on, having developed their skills, to become key speakers, certainly within their industry. The secret is in applying the rules and ensuring that you give your audience something new, something provocative, something challenging and above all, something entertaining.

Key Points to Remember

- Respect your audience.

- Celebrate your audience's achievements.

- Don't let your presentation become didactic and one-sided.

- Resist the urge to squash smart Alec questioners. Let your audience deal with them.

- Leave your audience on a high with some clear and inspirational calls to action.

- If you intend to use video or satellite treat it as a television appearance; television is a much more intimate medium than a large conference hall.

Appendix A

THE GOLDEN RULES

1. Give yourself time to prepare

2. Research your audience

3. Consult your colleagues

4. Play to the overlap

5. Prepare bullet point notes

6. Use prompt cards

7. Follow the Rule of Five

8. Allow one minute per card

9. Emphasise benefits, not features

10. Avoid acronyms and jargon where possible

11. Explain on first use if you need to use jargon

12. Use plain English

13. Use active not passive verbs

14. Avoid double negatives

15. Jokes — if in doubt, cut it out!

16. Visual aids must be "visual" and must be "aids"

17. Apply the necessary and sufficient test/the Fresh Fish Rule

18. You **must** rehearse

19. Arrive early and check the room and equipment

20. Project the right image for you and your organisation

21. Use de-stressing exercises if necessary

22. Ensure that your hands are in the home position

23. Start confidently — pause, eye contact, smile

24. Hit the ground running

25. Don't apologise, unless absolutely necessary

26. Be interactive

27. Respond to feedback

28. Choose appropriate gestures

29. Be yourself

30. End positively — summary, "what that means to you", call to action.

Appendix B

VENUE CHECKLIST

Even a perfectly prepared and well-rehearsed presentation can lose impact on the day if the logistics are not right. Here is a checklist of some of the points to look out for:

1. Meeting room

- Time of availability?
- Suitable size and shape?
- Suitable lighting?
- Can the room be blacked out?
- Can the lighting be dimmed?

2. Equipment

- Screen(s)
- OHP/slide projector:
  - ◆ Front projection?
  - ◆ Rear projection?
  - ◆ Standard Kodak carousel?
  - ◆ Is slide reversal/re-sequencing necessary?

- ◆ Spare bulbs?
- Tape/CD player
- Microphone(s):
  - ◆ For speaker?
  - ◆ For audience (if required)?
- Access to computer projection equipment:
  - ◆ Can one plug in own laptop?
  - ◆ Or simply bring diskette?
  - ◆ What presentation software programe?
  - ◆ Does host have computer support?
  - ◆ Back-up equipment in event of failure?
  - ◆ Power sockets and extension leads?
- Flip chart stand, paper, felt tip markers.

3. Miscellaneous points

- Coffee and refreshments for audience?
  - ◆ before? during? after?
- Reception table for registration and badging?
- Water jug and glasses for speaker(s)?
- Cloakroom facilities?
- Toilets?
- Rehearsal opportunity?
  - ◆ Ideally a time slot 4 x the length of the presentation?
  - ◆ Including visual aids and the technician who will be operating the equipment on the day?

INDEX

A

THE AZIZ
CORPORATION

The Aziz Corporation is Britain's leading specialist in spoken communications. Founded by Khalid Aziz in 1983, its consultants offer a wide range of spoken communication consultancy services ranging from tutoring for keynote speeches at international symposia through media training for television, radio and newspapers, to influencing skills and team briefings. The company comprises skilled consultants who apply The Aziz Corporation methodology in tailored tutorials designed to turn their clients into stunning speakers.

For more information, visit our web site www.azizcorp.com or email info@azizcorp.com. Alternatively telephone us at +44 1962 774766 or fax +44 1962 774728.